EBURY PRESS

TAKE YOUR TIME & HURRY UP

Joey Kidney is a creator, author, mental health advocate and entrepreneur. He began posting on YouTube in 2012 after he broke his leg during a hockey game. He had already suffered several concussions due to the sport, but in 2012, he decided to put his unfortunate circumstance to good use.

Joey saw almost immediate success posting weekly videos on YouTube, until he amassed a 7,00,000-subscriber base. He later found his way over to TikTok, gaining over 5.2 million followers and a new audience hungry for his content. He has 9,95,000 followers on Instagram, a large number of which are from the Indian subcontinent.

Joey highlights his journey, navigating the highs and lows of mental health, adulthood, being a dog dad and purchasing his first home most recently. He began writing his life story in 2017 and published his first book, *What's the Rush?*, in 2019. In 2021, he wrote his first poetry book, *Dreaming with My Eyes Wide Open.*

Joey has released several songs with Milestone, a collaboration with Matt Walden, gaining over 10 million plays on Spotify.

He has followed up *What's the Rush?* with *Take Your Time & Hurry Up*, which starts the next day, and continues documenting his life through the ups, downs and everything in between.

Take Your Time & Hurry Up

JOEY KIDNEY

EBURY PRESS
An imprint of Penguin Random House

EBURY PRESS

USA | Canada | UK | Ireland | Australia
New Zealand | India | South Africa | China | Singapore

Ebury Press is part of the Penguin Random House group of companies
whose addresses can be found at global.penguinrandomhouse.com

Published by Penguin Random House India Pvt. Ltd
4th Floor, Capital Tower 1, MG Road,
Gurugram 122 002, Haryana, India

Penguin
Random House
India

First published in Ebury Press by Penguin Random House India 2024

Acknowledgments

Maria, you are constantly inspiring me to continue to write just so I
can see your illustrations. You are beyond talented, thank you so
much for bringing this book to life.

Artist: Maria Melito

Nicki, you make me the writer that I am today. I owe a lot to
you for correcting my mistakes and making me look greater than I am.

Editor: Nicki Richards

10 9 8 7 6 5 4 3 2 1

ISBN 9780143463900

For sale in the Indian Subcontinent only

Printed at Replika Press Pvt. Ltd, India

www.penguin.co.in

This book is dedicated to...

(This was intentionally left blank so you can dedicate this book to someone you think will benefit from it. We're in this together, so I trust you to dedicate it to someone special.)

Love, j

Contents

October 20th, 2019

I am a confident, extroverted, emotional adult who continues to walk a path I'd just happened to stumble upon, a path that had light.

My name is Joey Kidney, and as I am writing this, I am twenty-three years old, and I am in New York City for the press tour of the launch of my first book. The universe has this crazy way of making our lives very complicated and truly unknowable as we continue on our path. We constantly think that we are going the wrong way, and the people that we encounter are not meant to be here, or they are meant to and we lost them. I am here to tell you: I am just as lost as you are.

Yet, I am here.

I am here with more questions about life, more concerns about my own, and more interest in others' lives. The one thing that is keeping us all here and curious is hope, and if you are someone that is in need of that, I truly hope that this book can help.

The last few years have been quite a ride, and I am still sitting here pondering why it all happened, as I am sure a lot of you are. We will constantly have questions every single day about why something happens and the way it did. It is not an issue to think like that, but it is very important to understand the way that it can positively affect your life. With the news, the media, and our own conscience distributing so much negativity, we can become blind to anything with light. For the past three years, I find the one thing that has gotten in my way the most has been myself. Putting yourself first is very important, but another very good skill to have is to let people in. That is a task that I am working on every single day, and it's something I figure I need more of in my life.

I hope this book makes you do one single thing, and that is:

FEEL.

I want you to open yourself up to what you are about to read, and be able to apply it. Whether to your own life, or to help someone that you love. Knowing that there are still people out there in the world that feel alone is the sole reason I am here writing this. I want to welcome you on my journey through happiness, pain, sorrow, light, darkness, and everything in between. My life is now yours, and I hope you can take whatever it is that you need from it, and borrow it for however long you want. This book is yours just as much as it is mine, and I truly hope it makes you FEEL because that is something we all need to do a lot more of lately.

This Feels So Good

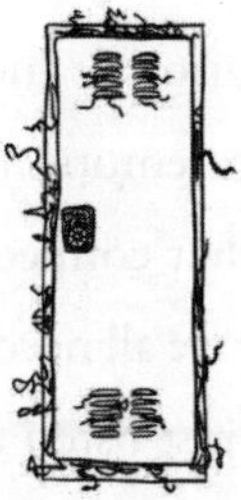

I grew up in an environment where it was considered "less of a man" to feel. To cry, to laugh, to feel emotion was something that you were humiliated for. I know this is not something that all of you can understand and I know some of you have experienced worse, but being a sixteen-year-old and growing up in a sports locker room wasn't exactly the most comfortable place. Being scared to talk about this topic is an understatement because I have felt traumatized for years. With the world and the people in it changing so quickly and mental health being talked about more, it is a difficult thing to adjust to, especially when we are used to believing and behaving a certain way. When we were all in the changeroom making jokes and being cruel to one another, it never occurred to us that we may have been offending someone.

The truth, however, was that there was definitely someone in that room feeling very judged, and we were all so oblivious. There is absolutely no excuse. In the end, we all left that room quite damaged. Whether it was the bully or the one bullied, we impacted every single life that stepped in and out of that room in a way that we never understood until now. Sometimes there is no apology that needs to be given because I believe there is a mutual feeling of discomfort as well as understanding from the outcome of a situation like that.

Sitting here now, I have never been more emotional, and more importantly, I am very proud to sit here and be emotional. Understanding what goes on in your head and what connects it to your heart is a very important skill that I believe we all need to pay attention to. I'd grown up always being told, "just listen to your gut" but never knowing what that means or the reasoning behind the decisions. On top of that, I was made fun of for even trying to feel.

The Universal Feeling

We are often told that love is a universal language, yet we forget that feeling unloved is just as well known.

The Demons I Don't Expect You to Understand

There are demons in all of us that we don't expect everyone to understand, whether it is not going to a party, canceling plans at the last minute, or laying in bed all day for a week. It is something that I never expect any of my friends or loved ones to understand, and it is not because I don't want them to think differently of me, it is simply because I don't have the energy to explain it. When I am debating talking to someone about something serious that is affecting me, I ask myself the question, "Do I want to answer two questions?" The majority of the time, my answer is no. There will always be a follow-up question when it comes to mental health, and I never have the energy to answer them because it is one of my triggers.To build up the strength and energy to do so takes a great amount of work and courage. I find my imposter syndrome kicks in and I immediately get hit with the thought that these feelings are not worth having. I know they are just questions that are meant to do more care than harm but sometimes diving into a problem that I don't know how to solve is terrifying for me. Especially when I don't think the person asking the question can solve it either. To build up the strength and energy to do so takes a great amount of work and courage.

Explaining my issue to friends is very difficult, and explaining why I didn't tell them before is even worse. I don't expect anyone to understand what I go through, even if that means ending up more lonely than I started.

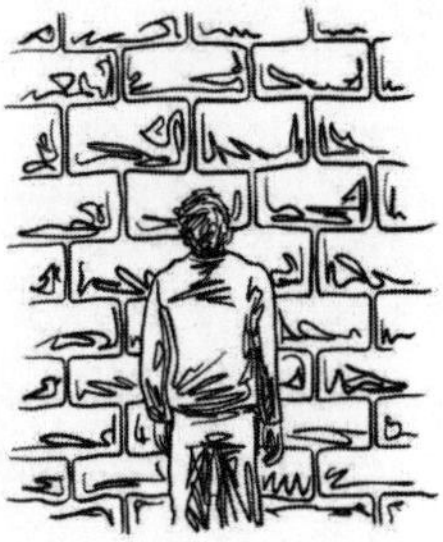

Recently, however, I found the courage to open up about my social anxiety. The character I assigned myself because of the job I do is just that, a character. It's not me. People think I am this outgoing person, and it is a very difficult thing to live up to when I have never been extroverted in my life. I have a very traditional friend group that truly doesn't "get out" often to experience the new changes in society, our world, and especially mental health because they are working hard at a job where mental health isn't necessarily talked about. But, I did it. I told them about my social anxiety, and their answer was "Okay, well, just let me know if you're coming to the party 'cause I am sure you will change your mind." Not that I was searching for a specific answer or reply, but let me tell you that this was definitely not it. They ignored how I felt and made me feel that I needed to change my mind. I felt unheard in this situation. I know it is a difficult thing to grasp for a lot of people, so I will not give up in trying to explain it to them, but for now, I will remain quiet and build up more strength.

Dear Reader Pt. 2

Over the past three years of my life that I have shared with you deeply, I have experienced pain, sorrow, guilt, sadness, happiness—basically every single emotion in the book—and the one thing I want to remind myself is:

I AM STILL HERE.

When we are experiencing any extremes in our mental illness, we always imagine the worst because how could you imagine anything positive in that situation? I also know that you are tired of hearing "it'll get better" or "it's going to be okay" or any other cliché phrase that people share with you when they don't know what to say. Let's be real, though—who would ever know what to say? There is some beauty in that because it means that no matter what, you are the master of your thoughts. You know what you want to hear, and you know what you want to do. It may seem very unclear at that moment in time, but that is when you ask yourself, "What's the rush?"

I am not here to tell you how to feel, or to tell you what you need to experience in life; I am just here to tell you to experience them. Be sad, get your heart broken, cry, laugh, be anxious, be nervous!

FEEL SOMETHING.

I want you to be able to experience things in life, and not limit yourself because you are scared of what might happen. You have already thought about the worst happening, so all that is left is the best.

Afraid of Falling in Love

Over the past few years of dating, I always thought that I never fell in love because I was never seeing the right people. The countless excuses of "oh, she's just not it" that I told my mom left her wondering if I was even trying to find the so-called "one." I think that we often create this invisible barrier where we are protecting ourselves from getting hurt, that sometimes we forget that we can avoid getting hurt all together.

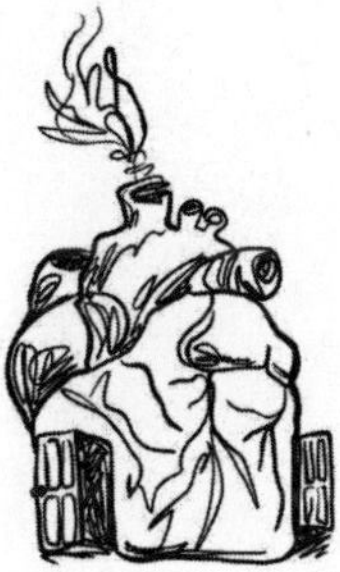

Being afraid of loving isn't always about letting someone into your heart, but it may be about the ones that have already left. When we come into this world, we are given people that we grew up loving, such as mother, father, brother, etc. For some, however, it is about the people we grew up to love. It happens to be quite different for many people because no love can be replicated, and once we feel a piece of love that later on leaves us, how could we ever settle for anything less than?

I think, for me, I am terrified of someone playing me like a game and humiliating me. Toying with my emotions and my heart to then leave me embarrassed and heartbroken as I watch them walk away. It isn't so much about being afraid to fall in love, but more being able to let myself fall without a rope holding me back because of my second thoughts. Falling in love is simply the best thing you can do, but what seems to continuously beat that is the act of letting yourself actually fall. To trust someone enough to allow yourself to let go and live a life with someone else.

Falling in love is not about being afraid of someone loving you, but it is about being not afraid to let yourself love.

For Those Not LookingFor Love

This is Joey (26yo) from the future coming back to add in an installment. In all my years of writing, my core theme has been that it is okay to be who you are and to fall in love with yourself and every part of your being. Throughout all of my writing, it's been easy to focus on finding love. But now as I'm getting a little older I've come to realize the greatest form of love that we can ever experience is the love we have for ourselves. In my first two books, I was writing many of my installments during moments where I felt most like me; moments when I was single.

I never realized how much the picture I tend to paint when I write is my life in search of love. Perhaps it's because I shy away from my own lack of self-love and I focus it on someone else. If I have somewhere else to put all this pain, heartache, and the feeling of being lost then I have more room for myself. When I write about finding someone, "the one", I've come to notice that most of the time I am writing about finding *myself*. If I'm being completely honest, my single years were some of the greatest years of my life, and that's not to downplay any of my relationships.

When I was single I was able to understand myself. What I liked, who I liked, and how I liked to be treated, and I was able to control whenever I wanted it to happen. I wasn't on the search for the perfect version of myself, I wasn't on the search for anyone to fill the void; I was just being me. Making mistakes, meeting new people, traveling around alone and discovering who I am without someone by my side.

I don't for a second regret finding the love of my life but I don't think I could have been the right partner for her if I didn't have those cherished experiences on my own.

Coming to the realization of who I really was happened to be a very difficult thing for me because growing up I never really fit in. I was a shy and introverted kid that came alive when I was spending time with people that I loved and felt comfortable around. Meanwhile, the people I was surrounded by were just natural extroverts that would always be people-pleasing with a smile on their faces. When I was single, I went back to being that same shy and introverted kid. That was a real standstill moment for me because I felt like I lost all my progress. But what I failed to remember is that the moments when I felt extroverted weren't when I was alone, they were when I was with people who made me feel comfortable. Ultimately, they were just people who would do all the talking for me so I never felt shy.

During this initial alone time, I did not have anywhere to hide or anyone to cover up my insecurities and that terrified me. I had to sit with myself and learn to simply be, without a mask, without covering anything up, without pretending. Eventually, I figured out my rhythm and understood who I was, instead of comparing myself to everyone around me, but until I did that work it felt like most of the time I was just pretending. I loved who I was with my friends but nonstop I would ask why I wasn't like them. Why did I not find love like them? Why could I not talk to people like them? Why was I not happy like them?

And even though these were just my friends and it had nothing to do with being single, it was something that I carried with me into my young adulthood. I was always on the search for people that would make me feel less introverted, and less shy because it was something that was always talked down on. So, after my first heartbreak, I was alone. I didn't want to be around anyone, I wanted to feel my heartache and I am glad I did because the moments after that changed my life.

Getting my heart broken wasn't an eye-opening experience; being alone was. Not searching for anyone, not trying to fit in, and not suffocating on the idea that I can't be me. I know what I like now, and I know how to respect that. When I go out to eat I ask myself if I want to eat with a fork and knife or with my hands and that determines my choice. I love going to a movie theatre with fully reclining chairs and I love it most while doing it alone. I love the fact that I don't like reading but love writing and no one is around me to tell me that is weird. I love ordering cold coffee, even in the middle of winter. I love being me and I love who I have become and I love the fact that I cannot wait to see myself change and evolve over the years.

After three years of being single, three years of learning about myself and embracing who I was, I found the love of my life.

I am not telling you that you shouldn't fall in love, I am telling you that you shouldn't be searching for someone to validate who you are. My partner loves how I choose my dinner selection, they don't get upset that I see movies alone, they love hot coffee and I love cold and most importantly they love me for who I am.

Being single isn't about being lonely, it is about being able to fall in love with yourself and enjoy every moment of it.

And now back to present day Joey.

A Way Out

Some people are so desperate for a way out that they pay attention to every single word, and once there is a wrong synonym, they call it out and escape the conversation. The idea of being uncomfortable and not being in control of a situation or their emotions terrifies them, whether it is their crush not liking them back so they pretend they never liked them, or when they fail a test so they brag to their friends that they didn't even study anyways.

I for one am not afraid of opening up; I am afraid of not receiving a reaction that gives me satisfaction. The response that I built up in my head before I even prompted a conversation. That is my constant way of life; waiting for a word to be said that I have already thought of in my mind.

What Is Love?

Love is kind,

Love is gentle,

Love is comforting,

But most importantly, love is curious.

I Am Ready

I am ready to fall in love

I am ready to dance like nobody's watching

I am ready to laugh so hard I pee my pants

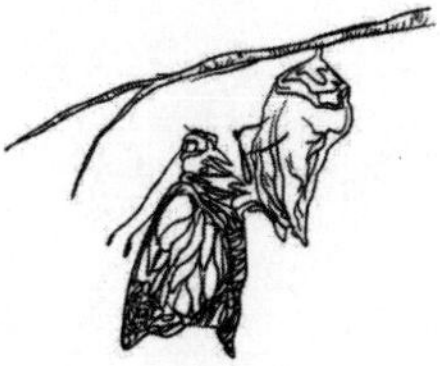

I am ready to woo the woman I love

I am ready to listen to you all predict that
what I am about to say follows with a but

And honestly, I thought it would too.

The pain, the sorrow, the falls were all followed with recovery, happiness, and ups.

It is finally time to move on, move forward, and do it all while being stronger.

After countless years of self-love, it is finally time.

I am ready to fall in love.

Dating Again

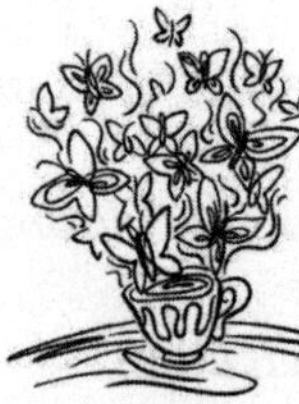

Three days ago I asked a girl that I truly love to be my girlfriend. Something that felt so right, yet the butterflies were just as real as the first time I sat down to have coffee with her.

Let's hope there won't be a "dating again" part two.

The Days of Nothingness

To all of my friends, I am known as the one that never stops working—the busy bee doing something that amazes others. There are days that are so action-packed I don't even get to sit down and really think about what happened. Days that just simply lead to burnout.

This was a common topic in 2019—the classic "burnout" of doing too many things at once. The thing that is not talked about, however, are the days that lead up to burnout. What I like to call:

The Days Of Nothingness.

These days are filled with plenty of things to do but with no motivation to fulfill them which leaves us feeling the urge to complete tasks even though we feel helpless while doing them. The classic "wake up and not get fully ready for the day until you absolutely have to," which leads to you being rushed and unprepared.

That description usually hits home with a lot of people because it is a very common feeling, and you don't need to have a lot of things on your plate in order to live through the days of nothingness. They truly feel like days that no one else lives through, but there are so many people out there stuck in this same rotation like this every damn day, wondering how to get out of it. Just like you.

The solution is quite simple, but the process is not the easiest, and that is:

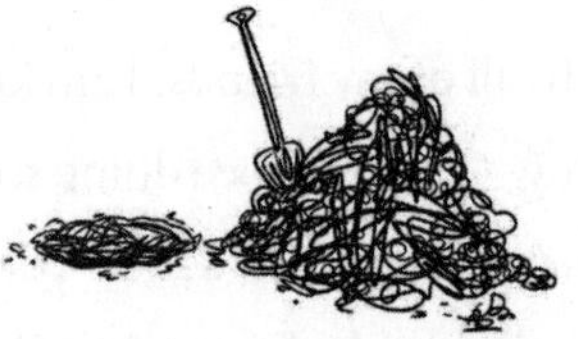

CHANGE!

Simply change your environment, your routine, and maybe what you are doing. I know we can really get caught up in our jobs and feel like we need to keep going and complete them fully, but sometimes we are just digging a hole to nowhere. Sit back and really look at your life and ask if it is going in the direction that you want most.

The days of nothingness don't always have to end in burnout, or start feeling frustrated and helpless. You can change them before you hit rock bottom.

When You Find That Person

One of the most difficult things about dating is that we are constantly trying to "find that person," that one person that is going to stop us in our tracks and change our lives and become our prince charming/princess. The problem there is that we never know when to stop looking for that One because we are always on the search. Each person we meet has the potential, but our mindset isn't on potential; it is on The One. Next thing you know, you are writing a "dating again" part five.

That is why they say when you are trying to find someone to love, you need to stop looking. If you are continuously looking, then you will never know when to stop because you don't want to miss the next best thing. But that best thing could possibly be right in front of you at this very moment, or it happened to be someone from a moment that you passed by so quickly because you were too busy looking for better.

People will tell you to stop looking like it is some easy thing to do when, in reality, we are all feeling quite lonely, and every time that new Christmas movie comes out, that loneliness begins to get a little stronger. This leads to the search becoming more in-depth with qualifications that are harder to meet. If I am here to be completely honest with you, I met my girlfriend while I wasn't looking, but the truth is that when you stop trying to find someone to love, you stop looking with your eyes and start searching with your heart.

There will always be a prettier person, but they won't always impact your heart the way that the One will.

When You Love Someone

You feel absolutely everything.

Every ounce of love, every hardship, every teardrop, every smile, and every ounce of sadness. This is also known as "baggage," which is an unfortunate term being spread by the ones that aren't truly in love. When you experience your loved one's pain for the first time, it leaves you feeling hopeless, knowing that you want to do so much to help but not knowing how. The little worries start to build up, and arguments start to ensue. It is in these moments that you realize your pain is no longer your own, that it is shared.

When your loved one is falling apart, so will you.

But I need you to remember that if you can't help in the big ways; I don't want you to feel guilty because there are plenty of small ways that have worked for me in my relationship.

I find we often forget how thoughtful it can be to send a morning text, grab someone's coffee for them, or even just a simple hug. Each person will have different requirements to get back on their feet, and as a loved one, you are the closest one that is able to help them when they need it.

I Don't Like Being Touched

I have never really met anyone like me, and I have never met anyone that truly understands what it is like to be me. And, well, I have never met anyone that does not want to be touched.

For starters, I have never gone to a doctor for this because I never really thought it was a bad thing, until I got to the age of having girlfriends, and I was doing a lot of things for the first time. Yes, I am talking about kissing and the whole birds-and-bees story. This was hard for me (no pun intended). You can only imagine me sitting down on the edge of the bed and telling the girl that was undressing herself that I didn't want to go through with it, and how fucking uncomfortable that would be.

However, my mother has always raised me to tell the truth and how it is important to remain true to myself. She did forget to include that I would experience utter embarrassment that made me want to die, yet here I am. You are probably wondering, *If you don't like being touched, then how do you get hugged or kissed or even do the nasty?* Well, folks, I don't always not want to be touched.

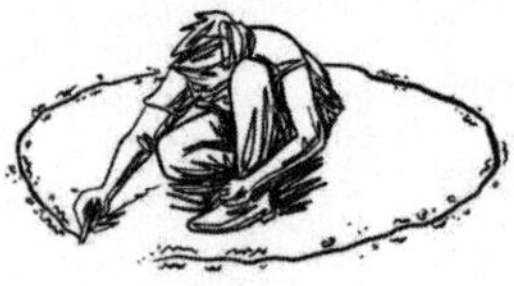

I have this window of opportunity when I feel like my most comfortable self. This window only opens once in a while, and usually right after I have drank water, exercised, and gone to the bathroom. To be honest with you, it opens when I have only thought about myself, even for just a few hours, and took action to take care of my health and well-being. Explaining this to a girlfriend or a hot date has always been the most difficult thing. I have tried every method, from telling them in the moment, pushing through and not telling them till the day after, and even trying to explain it before anything gets started. What is probably not hard to believe is that no one has ever understood what I was saying. No matter how much I explained it, no matter how many times I tried to make it easier, and no matter how many times I pushed through. I always feel like I am just better off living alone, where I don't have to explain my situation to anyone.

I think it partly stems from being anxious and combining that with my ADHD, but I really do not like to label things, so I tend to just separate it into its own category. For example, the other day I was watching a movie with my girlfriend, her all-time favourite, *Love Actually*. She got really upset that I did not want to cuddle, but what people don't see is how hard I am trying to sit still and not move. Having ADHD, I constantly want to get up, pace, and go do something. When someone tells me they want me to watch their favourite movie, I happen to take that very seriously, but I cannot sit still and be touched, all while paying attention to a movie.

I hope that maybe someone reads this one day and feels the same way I do; not because I would ever wish this upon someone, not because I would ever wish this upon someone, but just so we could know we're not alone.

To the Brown-Eyed Girl

To the brown-eyed girl that changed my life for the worse

You loved me, you made me feel like I belong, and you gave me hope

And at the time, that was the worst thing I could ever imagine

Because all I wanted to do was leave this world

And now I'm imagining a long-lived life on it with you.

Gravitate

You gravitate towards the future you want to have.

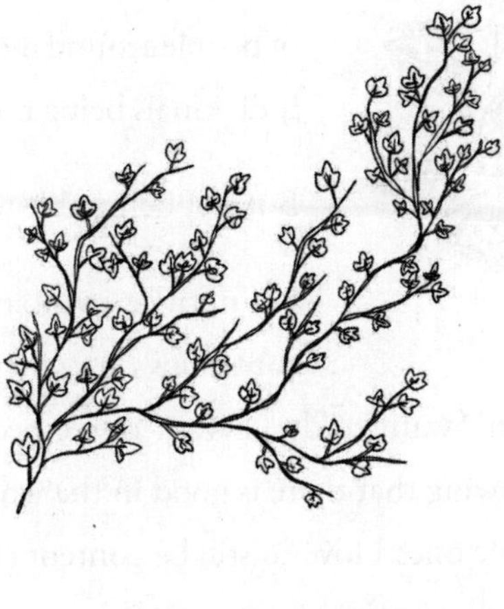

Seen & Invisible

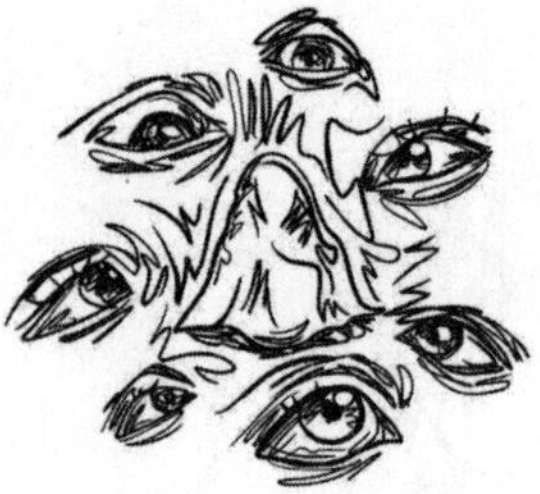

I always have this feeling of wanting to be in a big city, lit with the smiles of people around me, surrounded by individuals being themselves.

But not being able to be seen.

I want to be invisible while the world continues on, which I guess is just death, but I don't want to die. I want to see people living their happy lives, knowing that there is good in the world that is being spread. I want the ones I love to still be content that I am here so they are not sad that I am gone.

As I write this, I am in my favourite coffee shop called Ministry of Coffee, which turns into a bar during the late evening for all of the night owls. Each person in this shop is living their own life, battling their own demons, and going through barriers that I could never imagine facing myself. I think that is what makes each individual so strong because not one other person could ever live life at their pace.

We are all going through this life with a little invisibility cloak on because no one can see all of the battles that we are facing on the inside. So maybe I am already invisible, and I just think everyone is watching me all of the time.

I am seen and invisible.

A Work in Progress

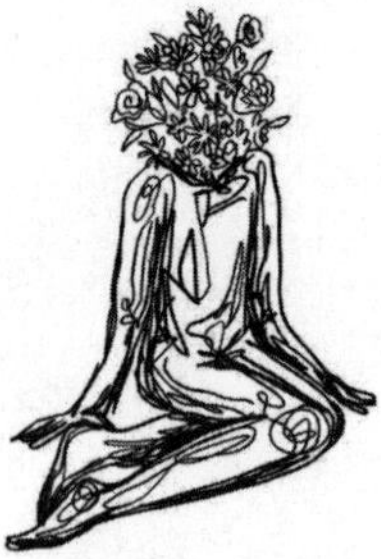

Our bodies will always be a work in
progress.

Not Being Here

I feel like not being here a lot of the time, but I don't want my loved ones to be sad.

Not dying, just not being here anymore.

I know you may read this and be sad or scared because it is a pretty shocking thing to hear. However, to someone who has been fighting to stay, I think it is a pretty comforting thought to have. Going to this place in your mind where all of the pain is gone, and no one is hurt. Everything is fine in this made-up, ideal world because all of your loved ones aren't hurt by your lack of presence.

I know I am supposed to be an author and write the way I feel here, but this is it.

This is all I have.

Sometimes the thought explains itself.

In the Real World

I asked my very close friend that I haven't seen in a while if he was dating anyone, or gone on any dates lately. He responded with:

"I went on an actual date like two weeks ago, and I hated it. She was into me—like, she really wanted to get to know me. And for some reason, I was like, online dating ain't it, or at least I had low expectations. Like I was just there thinking, in the real world, we would have never met. I wanna meet a girl that goes out and take pics or hangs with photographers or my friends. 'Cause then we would have something to build on. Like, I was just fishing for things to like about her. I felt really bad."

At first read, that may sound awful, but I have never been so proud of my boy. That feeling is a very hard one to grasp, especially while society is pushing online dating on us so often. Remembering who you are, and dating for reasons that are your own, is something that I believe everyone should remain close to.

Understanding what you like and not being cookie cutter is the best skill that you can have. It is not that you are avoiding the norm and being that cool kid, it is that you are finally realizing that you have interests and are attracted to certain things. You like what you like, and to be honest, I don't believe anyone should stand in the way of that, and you shouldn't settle for any less.

Missing the Love

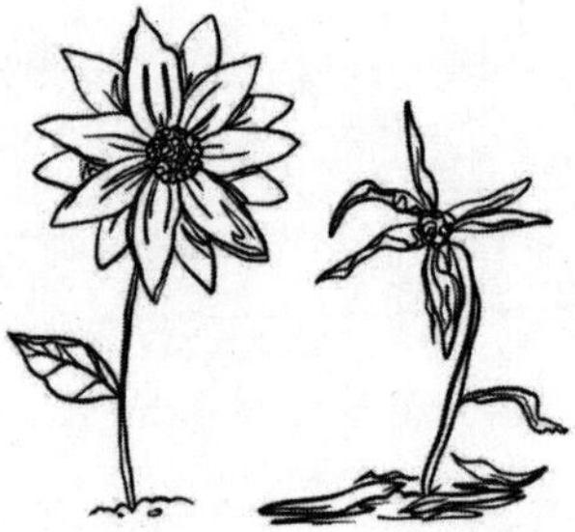

You're everything I've ever wanted, and I am not everything you need me to be.

Guilty Love

I finally got to the point where I have found someone who I believe I can truly love and fall for. This is a very rare feeling for me, or at least, I build it up to be like that in my head. I usually feel like I can't be loved, or when a bump occurs in a relationship that I am not worth it to even try. This dry, harsh feeling that I don't belong to anyone and I can never reciprocate the love that they need and deserve.

I feel awful and guilty that someone loves me so damn much, and I can't love them back. I can't even love myself.

I don't want to keep feeling like this. I want love, I want to be loved, and I want to love someone. But all I ever do is guide it into the ground in my deep, dark pit of depression with me. If you are reading this and you relate in any way, I want you to know that you are not alone and neither am I.

A Letter to My Ex-Girlfriend

To my ex-girlfriend,

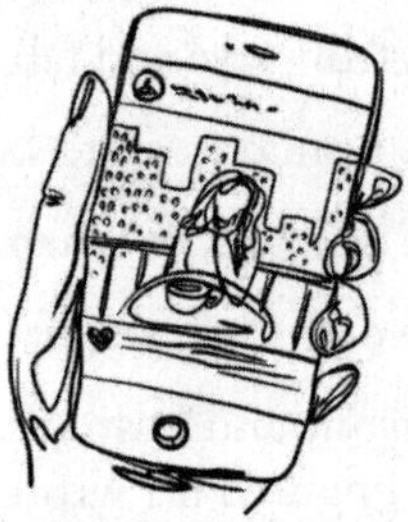

You look so happy without me

I'm not saying this as a diss, I am not saying this as a backhanded compliment

This isn't about a boyfriend or finding someone new, this is about you looking so damn happy because you finally found you.

Too Much Love

I used to believe that the reason I kept ending relationships was because I was incapable of loving someone. Until today, when I broke down over a little mistake my girlfriend made. Her mistake was loving me too much.

This is something that I have never been able to explain to anyone, but I figured if I wrote it down, it might make a little more sense, so here we go:

I feel so damn guilty when someone loves me because I can never give them the same amount of love back. Sometimes I feel like I am just overdosed with love from someone to the point where I cannot breathe and I need to just run away. It is the worst feeling in the world when the one you love makes you want to leave. And maybe it isn't love? Maybe it's just all in my head and I am truly incapable of loving someone. Or maybe this all does make sense and I just need to find someone to understand. Or maybe I am meant to be alone and have certain people come into my life every now and then.

I don't necessarily know what is wrong with me, but hopefully I am not alone in feeling this way.

How My Dog Changed My Life

April 13, 2019, was the day my entire life changed; it was the day that I went to pick up my puppy, Frankie.

After three years of research on Australian shepherds, and finding a proper and respectful breeder, it was finally time to change my life. A lot of people get dogs simply to get a cute dog, but I wanted a dog to change my life. I was ready for my entire life to take a turn for the best. For dealing with anxiety attacks and depression spells, Frankie was meant to be more than a pet from the start; he was meant to save my life. Now, that is a lot to put on an animal when I don't even know how they are going to act, or their personality type, but let me put your mind at ease and spoil it a little bit because it was a perfect match.

I was able to get Frankie at eight weeks old, but the breeder gave owners the chance to meet the pups at four weeks old just to see what you were getting yourself into. Unfortunately, I was travelling at the time and wasn't able to go and visit him at that age. The breeder kept telling me that he had the perfect temperament, but his proportions weren't perfect for him to be a stud dog, which was the reason that I was able to bring him home. That being said, the breeder was amazing with how she handled her business because she never treated it as such. These puppies weren't simply a purchase; they were a part of her life.

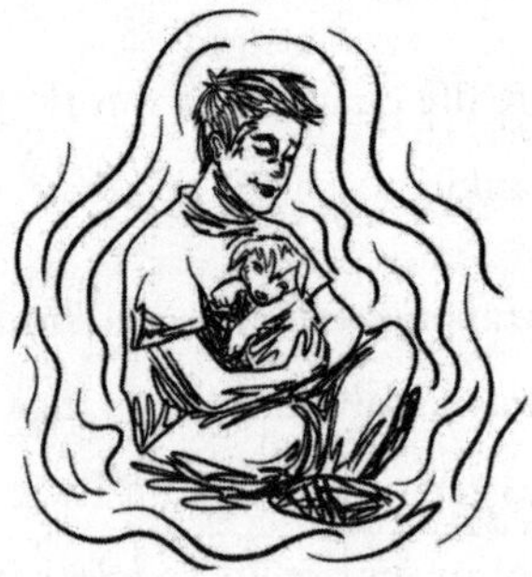

The day finally came to pick up Frankie. I brought my dad along for the ride because I wanted to snuggle Franks on the way home, but the main reason I asked him to come was so he could tell me if I was making the right decision. There is a very high chance that a puppy won't want to go home with you, even if you want it, and I wanted my dad to be there to be able to break the news to me if there was any. We pulled up to the breeder's cottage, and I immediately started getting emotional walking up to the door.

I had only seen pictures of him, and he had definitely never seen me before, but when I opened that door, the first thing I saw was him amongst twelve other puppies. I don't know if it was just a coincidence or a sign, but our eyes locked and he started running right towards me. We had a connection immediately, but I didn't want to overthink it and believe something that wasn't true, because they were puppies and maybe they were all looking at me and I only noticed Frankie.

As it turns out, I wasn't overthinking it. We went outside, and I sat on the floor of the deck as all of the puppies surrounded me. Frankie was trying to come up to see me, but he couldn't make it because of the swarm of puppies that were peeing, pooping, and drooling all over me. So what did he do? He waited patiently. And after ten minutes, all the puppies were asleep on the deck, all tuckered out except one. Frankie was on my lap, in my arms, and looking directly into my eyes. All of this was happening as the breeder said, "I have never seen one of my dogs choose someone more than Frankie chose you. This is a true connection."

And she didn't have to say that to me—I was already sold when I put the deposit in eight months prior—but hearing it melted my heart. I have never felt more complete than when I had Frankie in my arms on the drive home. However, I feel what people don't talk about enough is how fucking scary it is. I am now the life support for this animal; they have no chance of making it without me. I am their everything, and I need to make that feeling mutual. Even though I was scared, I was excited, I was pumped, and I finally felt like I had filled a void in my life.

Now, I know that when you buy a dog, you buy a heartbreak, but Frankie will be worth the pain at the end because the journey has been oh-so-sweet. Fast forward a year, and Frankie has been an absolute saint. I do put a lot of work into training, but he is mindful, respectful, and he treats me how I treat him. He has been everything I have ever wanted him to be and more. I am one of the weird people that don't really care for puppies because I was so excited to have a dog that followed commands and understood life and their purpose. It took Frankie one day to understand his. I am not his dad, he is not my son; we are in this together as brothers, and learning as we go.

He helps me tremendously with my mental health, including my anxiety, depression, ADHD, and even suicidal thoughts. When I am anxious, he hugs me. When I am depressed, he licks my face, grabs a toy, and excites me. And when I am feeling like I want to end it all, he only has to be present and I remember that life is worth so much more than ending it early. I didn't have to teach him the majority of these things because animals can sense your energy; you just need to open up to let them feel it. The day I opened up my heart to my dog is the day when he started to trust me with everything he was scared of.

Now, if you are thinking that every story is like this, I'll tell you right now that it is not. Even though Frankie has been amazing, it has been a tremendous amount of work. With all this work that has been put in, the return has definitely been greater. If you are thinking about getting a puppy—or more specifically, an Aussie—then you need to understand that they aren't high energy, they are just smart and don't want to sleep all day. Treat them like you would treat a human baby, treat them like you'd treat yourself, treat them with love, kindness, and respect, and I promise you will create a wonderful bond and have an amazing little floof.

Feeling Scared

Imagine waking up in a world that terrifies you, a world where something new burns down every time you blink. Well, in the year of 2020, this became our world. It leaves you feeling hopeless in your actions and doubtful in your future because you are waking up with the fear that you won't tomorrow, that you may not even want to.

Feeling scared is an understatement of how I have felt over the course of this year so far. Hopeless, stupid, uneducated, wrong, depressed, suicidal, and the list goes on, but none of it will be good, so let's skip to the end. Growing up, I never imagined living in a wartime, or being scared to go outside, or let alone watching the world burn from the inside of my apartment. Things needed to be changed in the year of 2020, and the world was willing to sacrifice lives in order to do it.

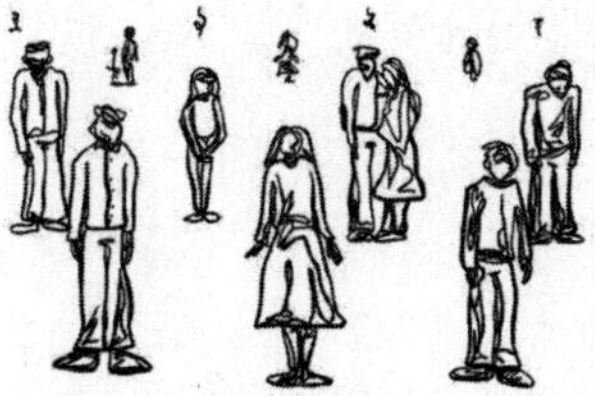

At first, I was terrified and I didn't understand, but as time went on and the stories came out, I started reading and being able to feel the world's pain. A lot of hurt goes on that we do not see. No matter where you are from in the world, the colour of your skin, or the religion you believe in, there is always something terrible happening out in the world that needs change. In the beginning of all of this, I was very selfish because I thought, "Oh, it isn't happening to me, so I am safe." But let me tell you this: if you were watching the buildings burn, the people dying, and love being lost, you'd start to care as well.

And from this day on, I vow to always play my part and be willing to learn when the education is at hand. Not only does it better my life, but it can help save one in the future as well.

I Feel So Alone

This is a feeling that I thought I would never feel again.

I feel like my problems aren't as big as my friends.

I feel alone.

I feel scared.

I feel dead.

2020

A year that changed everyone's life for better and for worse—the year of the pandemic.

My last instalment was written three months ago, and the world has been in the same place. My words are stuck in the same spot, and my heart hasn't beaten since. I can't help but struggle with writing this piece because I don't believe my opinion is with the majority.

The world finally slowed down for me, and for the first time in my life, I felt myself live. Every friend, family member, pet, and even stranger was going through the exact same situation as I was. Complete and utter lockdown. No moving, no loving, and definitely no touching. A world that was seeing so much hate and anger towards one another was finally put in the same situation. I felt the whole world stop.

As someone who doesn't like being touched, this was a gift. As someone who faces a lot of anxiety about the future, this was a gift. But as someone - like everyone who faces illnesses, this was a curse.

COVID-19 changed all of our lives in both positive and negative ways. The downside is quite obvious, and I am not here to write a news article. I believe that it really opened our eyes to the way we were all living. It allowed us to stop and really see the hard truth of how our lives were at home and gave us the opportunity to adjust how we lived. One of the things that I noticed I needed to change was the way I was breathing. I know it may be a very weird thing to notice first, but I think it was an underlying issue that led to a lot of other problems.

My breathing was off because my head and my heart were going in two different directions. I was watching the world move faster and faster, and I was trying to catch up by running in circles. In reality, I just needed to understand that I was meant to go a different way. I started working out, I started looking at food as something to enjoy instead of good and bad, and I began to breathe. This may sound very dramatic for some, but I believe there is one person reading this that can relate to every single word. The world finally stopped moving and allowed me to not only catch up but to realize my own path was going in a different direction. I started following that path at my own speed, and it changed my life.

And for that, 2020 was the best worst year of my life.

You Were Born to Stand Out

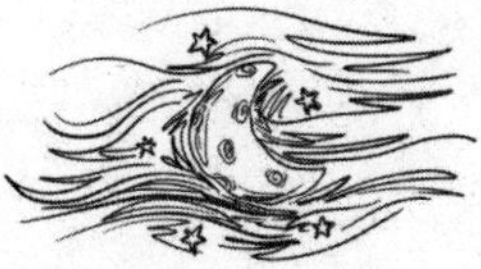

This is a line that may help a lot of people, but it truly pains me because I am shy, I am introverted, and I have never wanted to stand out. And when I am this way, when I feel like I don't belong, like I don't fit in, and I get the advice of "you were born to stand out."

It hurts me even more because my entire life I have wanted to fit in and feel like I belong. I have felt this way ever since I was eight years old, and now I am twenty-four and I finally feel loved and happy and accepted. And it is because I finally fit in. I fit into my body, I fit in with the right friend group, and I fit in with this world.

I stopped "trying to stand out" because I was born to, and I kept doing me and the right people came along. So if you are reading this and you need others, please don't give up...

They are on their way.

Resolutions

Let's make this the first year we stop making resolutions for things we hate doing.

If you don't like reading, don't vow to read a specific amount of books.

If you hate working out, don't hate yourself when you don't do it.

Instead, listen to an audiobook, eat healthy, and if you struggle with self-love, I encourage you to stop seeking external validation from people who don't love you.

Your resolutions shouldn't be things that depress you, they should be things that encourage you to wake up every day and *live*.

Another Life

When we look into the future

We look at a better and happier life

The sun shines a different shade

Without a cloud in the sky

Everything seems to be so clear

Another life tends to seem so peaceful

Less worries and less heartbreak

No pain in sight and no hurt in mind

That is, until we get to the thought

That this may have been our other life

This was everything we hoped for

And dreamed of

Everything just became so unclear

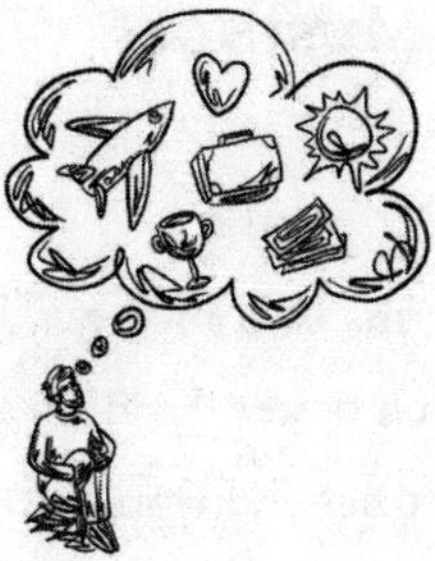

Another Life: Musings

Imagine thinking in terms of tomorrow. Imagine thinking, "Another life will be so much better. I can't wait until my other life or this other life. If I was a teacher, I would do this, or in my other life, I would want to be this so I could be happier. I would be happier if I had one more life. I would do it all over again."

My thought process about this is what if this is our other life? What if this is our doing it all over again? So I think we should cherish what we have right now. I think that's what we need to do. We need to love the life that we are given, and if you want to be a teacher, if you want to go explore the world, then I say fuck it. Go do it! You know there is no one in this life that's going to lecture you, that is going to tell you, "Oh, just do it." Well, here I am, telling you to do it!

Don't wish away today, because today is a great day.

The New Year

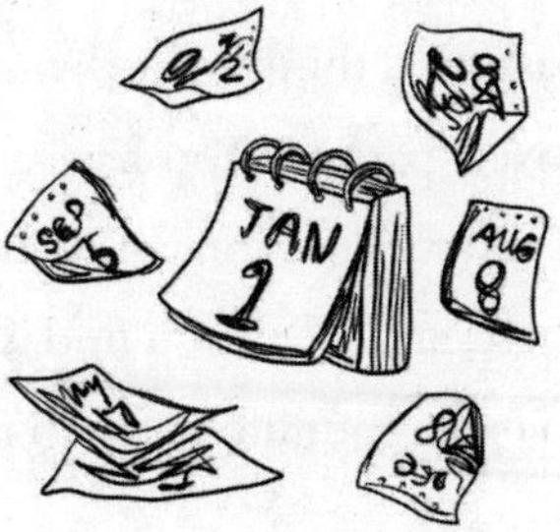

I don't think of the years as years, I don't think of a birthday as getting older, I don't think about any of that. I don't measure the passing of time in anything larger than days. It's just a year, just a calendar flip. We put so much pressure on a new start that we forget to enjoy what we are living right now! We forget to enjoy all the little things.

Passion And Purpose

Do you think it is important to have a purpose in life or find a passion? I think you're living a life that's not fair to you if you don't have a passion. You have a purpose in this life, and it's to live it. You have a passion in this life, even if you have not found it yet. It's there, and when you find it, you need to take it and go. It is going to make your life so much more exciting.

I don't think we are in this life just to become a world leader or a doctor. I think we are in this life to wake up every single day and be happy and enjoy the life that we have, whether it is by being with someone or doing something we love. When you find that passion, you are going to be so happy.

I promise you. I promise you it is there. I promise you that you have it.

Managing to Love Someone for a Long Time

We sometimes ask ourselves, "Can I love this person for *x* amount of years?" In order to love somebody else, we always hear that we have to love ourselves first, right? But it doesn't go like that. It doesn't actually work like that.

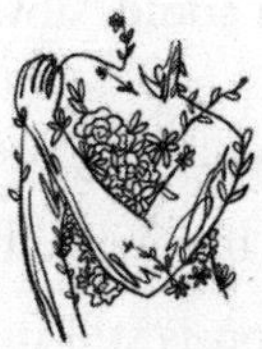

Yes, we have to love ourselves first, but we also have to love ourselves always! We have to be first always! No matter how many people are in your life—no matter if it is your mom, your dad, your girlfriend, boyfriend, whatever it is—you have to put yourself first all of the time. You need to take care of yourself first all of the time. You are going to take care of yourself, which will allow you to be okay and ready to take care of somebody else.

Dating the Right Person

I don't think we ever know we are dating the right one. Because there is always going to be somebody better, there is always going to be somebody with nicer hair or bluer eyes or a nicer smile. Everything. There's always going to be someone better, and I think that you just have to be happy with where you are and appreciate what you have instead of trying to replace the good in your life for what could "always" be better.

Stop putting pressure on someone else, and truly look within to find if you are happy. Once that question is answered and this person is still in your life, then you'll know they're meant to be there. If you are happy within, you will be able to be happy for the ones around you.

Seconds of Bad Thoughts

Have you ever had an amazing day be ruined by the slightest of bad thoughts? Me too. So here is what I want you to do.

I want you to write them down below.

Now, in thirty seconds, come back to this. Look above and read about the little bad thoughts that ruined your day. I want you to read it out and listen to yourself say them. And if you feel up for it, beside them I want you to write the positive version of the thought. I think it is important to think about the good, the bad, the ugly, and the beautiful of everything. What this does for me is it allows me to disassociate my feelings from the subject. Allowing me to have a different point of view that can help me move past it.

Overthinking

Take a break. Please.

We can all overthink, it's not hard. That is not a talent of yours. Know what is really cool? When we think about something we love. When we think about something we really enjoy doing, when we just take a break and we are in our own thoughts, when we are just so obsessed with what we are doing.

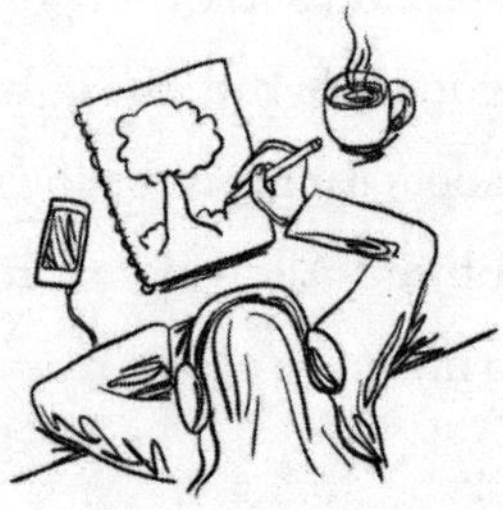

That is fucking cool. I want you to think about something that you truly love doing where your thoughts disappear. When I sat down to write this, I had a hard time coming up with one.

So to help you out, I will tell you mine. When I am playing hockey, the whole world disappears. When I am sipping on an iced coffee, my mind goes blank for a moment. When I am laughing so hard that I am about to cry, I forget all the bad things in my head.

When we think about these things, when we take a break from the negativity, it is almost like it generates a whole new channel of thoughts.

No Friends

The feeling of being lonely and the thought of having no friends when you are surrounded by them tends to be overwhelming. Especially in the year of 2020, the year of the pandemic. We are stuck at home and all alone—heck, how can we *not* think we have no friends? I have felt this way a lot recently, and instead of really trying to value my friends, I tried more to value myself.

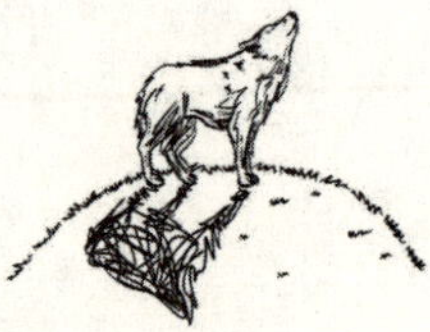

I was always complaining about how I had so many friends but that I didn't feel like I did, and that's very normal. I learned to value my alone time more than I do time with my friends. And I cherished my friendships a million times more because I wasn't craving them. I don't need them, I wanted them, and that is a huge difference. You will value the ones you love a lot more when you value yourself.

Moving Home

I am currently writing this on February 2, 2021, and I am in a place I have never been. A new home. With a global pandemic taking over the world and a work-from-home order taking place, my roommate and I decided that we needed a bigger space. The place I left was a home that I moved into because I wanted change from a spot in my life that I couldn't handle anymore. I know they say that running away from your problems is never good, but it was the only thing I could do when waking up every day reminded me about how much I didn't want to wake up.

That might be a little dark for some, but it truly made me understand that I deserve better, that I deserve a place that feels like home. A spot that makes me happy every single day to wake up and live my life. That place was the apartment that I moved out of this year. Now I am in an actual home, and no, I did not buy it. Everyone around me has been yelling at me to buy a home and invest in property to make money and gain equity. To be honest, that sounds like a headache and unhappiness all in one sentence. All I wanted was to wake up in a spot that inspired me to live and actually be happy without thinking about the debt that I need to pay off and how if it all goes wrong, that I have to be the one to fix it.

So maybe I didn't make the best financial choice in renting a new home, but who is to decide what the best choice for my well-being is? All of my friends? My mom? My dad? All wrong, because the answer is me. If you are reading this and you are in your twenties or younger and people around you are encouraging you to grow up faster so you won't make the mistakes that they did, then listen closely. You will make mistakes. It is inevitable, and it is not a bad thing no matter how you look at it. There will always be those times where we'll look back and wonder how something would have ended up if we'd done it all differently. There will be those times where we would have chosen a different direction on our path. We can sit here and wonder all we want, or we can accept our choices and move on.

I am happy in my new home, no matter what my friends or peers say about it. I wake up happy. Do you?

Loving You and Feeling Guilty

I have come to the realization that I have trouble loving, and the worst part is that I don't know why. It isn't that I haven't tried figuring it out, it isn't that I was hurt in the past; I just do not know why. I know you are probably thinking, "Well, maybe you're with the wrong person." And that is a valid statement, but I don't believe it to be true. I have so much love and compassion for the person that I am with, but when I think about doing something loving and kind, I always find myself feeling a little guilty.

Valentine's Day is coming up, and last year I absolutely crushed it by doing some very thoughtful things. This year, well, not so much. I can blame the pandemic all I want, but I generally just felt unmotivated. It's not because the love for my significant other is not there, I just find myself comparing everything to what I did in the past and digging this hole of guilt deeper and deeper. The thoughts that come to my mind during this process are as follows:

"Maybe I am not good enough?"

"I don't deserve their love."

"Maybe it is just better to break up so they aren't upset with me."

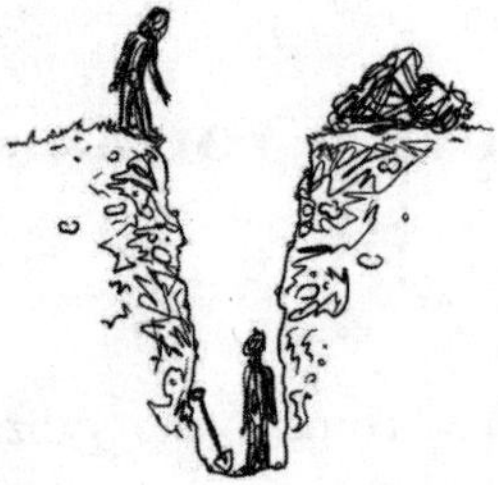

This all goes back to growing up very insecure and lacking self-confidence. I always hated individual sports; I was a team player because the total blame couldn't be placed on me. I would put myself in the position to quit before I could fail so I didn't look stupid. And now that I am writing this, I am thinking that maybe I shouldn't be. You are reading this thinking I am some awful person with no heart, but I want you to realize it is the exact opposite. As I sit here feeling bad for myself, I am trying to figure it out at the same time.

Why do I feel so guilty for loving someone?

Is it because they love me more than I love them?

Or is it because I don't deserve their love?

And in my mind, those aren't exactly the most positive thoughts. It isn't that those thoughts are right, but it is that those thoughts are more one-sided than anything. Maybe the reality of it is more like this:

Is it because I have a lot going on and I forget that someone loves me for me?

These feelings are valid, so why do you feel bad for feeling them?

You're still in love—you just need to realize it.

And these thoughts may still not seem very positive to you, but to me, there is hope. Finding and discovering who I am is a lifelong journey, and if I could sit here and answer all the questions that life has to ask me, then I'd be better off not living this life at all because there would be no enjoyment.

When I'm battling with the thoughts of feeling too guilty to love, I ask myself this one question: "Do I love them?" It's a question that seems simple, but it always gets me thinking. We all know that relationships take a lot of work and effort, but if you don't love them in the first place, then maybe you need to have some important conversations.

Why Are We Always Sad?

I think a lot about why we are so comfortable when feeling sadness, and it has taken me years to figure it out for myself. It would leave me lying awake at night, trying to find the missing figure in the equation, as if our feelings can be solved by a calculator. We go to school and we feel empty. We go to a party and we feel invisible. We are with our friends and we feel lonely.

What is something that all of those have in common? They involve us feeling something.

When we go about our day, we are experiencing life as usual. In someone else's eyes, we are normal and doing just fine. To the outside observer, we are enjoying life to the fullest and getting by each and every day with enough money in the bank and a smile on our face. But in reality, they are looking at a ghostly figure. Someone that hasn't felt something since the moment they opened their eyes when they woke up, someone who is simply sleepwalking through their day.

I am no doctor, I am no scientist, but after studying my own personal feelings and experiences, I realized that I was always sad because that was the only thing I was capable of feeling, and feeling sad was better than feeling nothing. I allowed myself to feel—to feel pain, to feel tears, to feel something . . . to feel anything. And it became a vicious cycle of waking up dreading life and waiting for the moment I could be sad again. This isn't who my mom raised, this isn't me. I used to be such a happy kid, and that is what confused me the most.

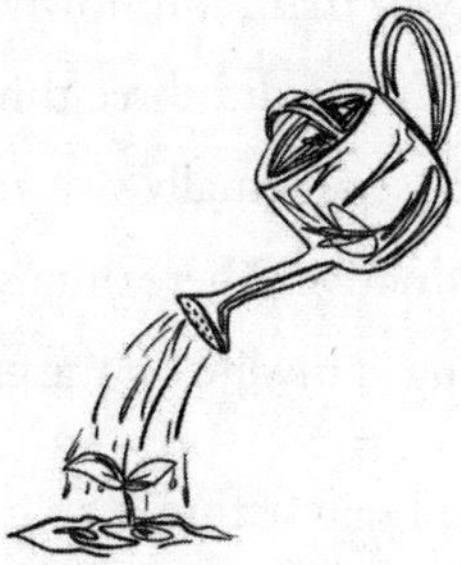

So I made the change. The amount of days where I would wake up not feeling energized, or I would wake up tired, are too many to count. Those are all days where I would just wait it out and hope the evening would come quicker so I could feel something and gamble on the next day. This wasn't a life that I wanted to live, so I started making little changes.

You can watch a million YouTube videos about someone's 5 a.m. morning routine, but that is not real life. That is the edited version of someone. Over a few months, I noted down the things I ate, the activities and things I did, the people I saw, and how my days ended. Now, I am not going to tell you that I have it all figured out and I have a to-do list when I wake up like a robot. But I can tell you that I am slowly getting happier and happier each time I wake up. I did three things: ate whole foods (and enough food), exercised (actually sweated), and did something that made me feel productive. These things that may not seem big to some absolutely changed my life on the greatest of scales.

Like I said before, I do not have it all figured out, and personally I don't believe that we should. If we did, then we would never mess up, we would never be sad, and we would never be able to feel again.

Happiness is a choice. Sometimes, sadness is too.

A Trend of Emotion

It is time to make some blood boil, and I know it will because I got furious when I asked myself this question. At what point is my sadness becoming a trend? Listen, I am not saying depression doesn't exist, I am not asking you to stop the pain you are going through. It is a question that I once asked myself, and I was surprised by the answer. After years of always going through something and always making it out, I failed to realize how strong I'd become.

Before, a simple phrase worded the wrong way would set me off, and now I just reword it in my head so I can provide a better response than the way they originally said it. I would get so upset if someone didn't respond to my text, and now I just call them instead. I would actually have a full-on panic attack if my picture on Instagram didn't get enough likes as the last one, and now I just post what I love.

You see, I found myself in this rut of falling into sadness because it worked that one time. Someone would respond to a sad text a certain way that would make me feel wanted, or a video with sad puppy-dog eyes would get me more views. And subconsciously, I would just repeat this method every single day without even realizing it until after it stopped working, and I fell into the vicious cycle of asking myself why. I kept falling into this rut because when things went bad, I would let go of my strength and do what was easy.

But if you know me, then you know the saying that comes next . . . everything is easier said than done! So to conclude this little mind burst of an instalment, I realized that being sad became something I slowly got addicted to, and whenever something would go wrong, instead of solving it, I would just be sad instead. And you might be thinking, "I am in that spot too, how do I get out of it?" The way that I found a way out was allowing myself to take a second and slow down. I always felt guilty for doing this because it felt like life was constantly moving, but when things didn't go my way or the sun didn't rise the next day. I took a moment to allow myself to feel. I replaced the thought of "this made me sad", with the question of "why do I feel sad about this?" And oftentimes, I found myself coming back with a different answer and that was all because I made it okay for myself to take time and think, feel and even if it was just one extra second, it changed my life.

Things Just Get Better

Growing up, I always wanted to die. I would make up stories in my head of me having cancer, or getting in a car crash, or just ending it all. And as I am typing this, I am almost in this hysterical mood because I can't believe that I once wanted to end it all when life could be so good.

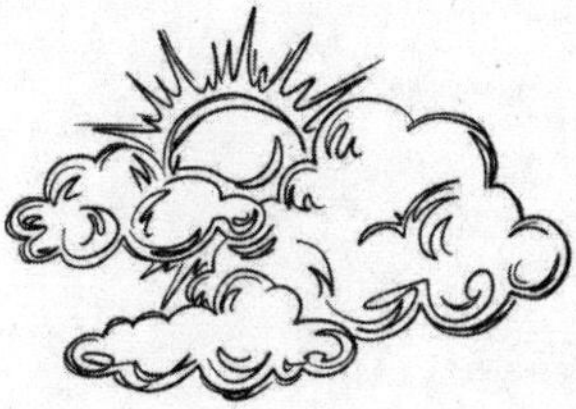

I am twenty-four years old as I write this, turning twenty-five next month, and I just don't want to die anymore.

Did life get more enjoyable? Did I just stop giving a shit about what some random person thinks about me? Did I realize that I won't even remember that person in five years? Did I learn that maybe my problems aren't as big as the world's?

I know everyone hears this all the time, but it's true. If you are reading this and you are struggling . . . it gets better. I wish I could explain it, but I just need you to trust me. It somehow gets better. And I think the best part is not knowing how because it is different for each one of us, which I have explained my story in this book and I cannot wait to hear how it gets better for you.

Allow Yourself to Miss Out

I think we don't give ourselves the time off that we deserve. This can be from school, work, relationships, or even just our daily routine. We work at them so much and so far in advance that we have our next fifty-two weeks planned out and nothing can change that. And that is great, but those plans will switch up because change is inevitable.

Consider not having coffee tomorrow, canceling dinner plans, or being a little late to see friends. Miss them, miss something, miss out on fucking breathing for a beat.

Okay, I know I may have lost you on that last one, but continue reading and I will make up for it.

How do we know we like something? It isn't really ever in the actual moment. Yes, maybe we get a little spark of excitement, but the true moment that we realize we really enjoy something or someone is when we are away from it. Taking a break and missing out doesn't mean that you care less, it doesn't mean that you hate yourself, it doesn't mean anything negative when your heart is in the right place. I remember that in the middle of my relationship, I was really struggling to stay in love and I could not figure out why. I was spending every single day with the person, I was glued to them and laughing and enjoying the moments . . . Until I wasn't.

So I took a break and I took my time off and something magical happened. I fell in love with the feeling. My feeling. Not the feeling of missing out but the feeling that is truly deep in my chest—not just the one on the surface that comes out when they are around. I fell in love with every aspect of missing someone, missing how I felt with them, who I was with them and the moments we had together.

I am telling you this so you understand that just because you take breaks does not mean that you are quitting or weak or a coward. It means you are growing stronger, you are listening to how you feel and you are learning how it is to miss something that you love.

Dear Reader

Lately I have been speaking with one person and one person only: myself. I find it hard to sit here and imagine that I am talking with someone else when the world that I seem to be living in tends to reside in my head. I have this inner dialogue—well, I guess it's more of a monologue now that I think of it. I can't help but wonder if there are those reading who may be feeling the same exact way. If so, this goes out to you.

All of those who talk more to themselves than anyone else, not because they feel alone but because they actually enjoy the conversation. Allowing yourself to ask the correct questions and check in with yourself and how you are feeling versus waiting for someone to come along and fulfill the self therapist need. But do you actually realize that you are not alone? I know I have said it before, and I know you have heard it before, but do you actually believe it? This book isn't just "relatable." The reason why it hits home in certain areas is because I am human, and so are you, and we go through life. We are a lot more common than everyone tends to think because I find that we all like to be our own person and we try our best to not copy trends because we want to stand out in some way.

I don't want to discredit you, or take away any unique value from your life, but you and I are quite similar. You and another stranger reading this are quite similar, and that may sound creepy, but I find there is a fine line between comfort and discomfort. Once you merge those two, I think the world tends to seem a little more peaceful.

My Birthday

Last year, I hated it. The year before that, I hated it. Five years before that, can you guess? I hated it. But this year just felt different, and I don't know why. I have my suspicions, but the only way for me to figure it out is to write it down. You see, a lot of us know our answers before we ask the question; we just want an excuse to be wrong so we can feel sorry for ourselves in order to feel something.

When my birthday rolled around this year, I'll be honest—I forgot about it. Especially with the global pandemic still majorly impacting everyone's lives, there was much more on people's minds than my birthday. Not that I want people to have my birthday on their mind—or maybe I do, but I definitely don't want to celebrate. Or maybe I do?

I have always hated my birthday for the sole purpose that I don't like the way people treat me and how it makes me feel. Guilt surrounds me throughout the entire day with thoughts like "oh, I didn't get them a present" or "they should be having a special day too." I have always felt like I did not deserve it, and it was easier to hate it than it was to mask my feelings and put a smile on my face like everyone else wanted.

I have a balloon beside all of my social media handles, and not because I am a huge *IT* fan. It is because I believe everyone should live every day like it is their birthday. Every single day on this Earth should be special, not just the day that you came into it. And maybe that is why I finally feel okay on this day. Because for once in my life, I finally feel like I spent the year being one hundred percent myself and doing things to make myself proud to be here. I can't really remember a day of the year where I was truly upset with my actions, or where the depressed devil in my head was telling me to go die. I worked hard on my mental health, my physical health, and my relationship with my family, friends, and girlfriend.

All in all, I think I actually did not mind my birthday this year for a few reasons:

1. There was a global pandemic to distract everyone.

2. People cared more about Earth Day this year because they felt bad for ordering too many Amazon packages.

3. I finally accepted who I am and cared for myself.

And I don't know about you, but that sounds like the greatest gift you could ever receive. I am grateful to be alive, I am happy to be here, and I am happy to share this message with you. But who knows—maybe I'll hate it again next year.

The Simple Method

In the past two years, I have realized several things, I have unlearned a tremendous amount, and I have adapted to the conditions that life has thrown at me. But the one thing that always intrigued me when I looked at those around me who were successful, was asking, "How did they do it?" I found myself stuck not understanding how someone found their passion, hustled, and achieved. So what is the key?

Stop giving a shit.

You're probably thinking, *Oh, wow, you think you're a genius, eh?* But hold on. We always hear the saying "stop caring about what others think," and even though this is important, it is not the key to moving on and building success for yourself. I mean to stop caring what *you* think. Countless times during the day I find myself listening to my inner thoughts about what I need to do or should be doing. Thinking about myself and how hurt I will be when I find out what other people think of what I do. I am not thinking directly of others, I am thinking selfishly and really standing in my own way.

For example, take this book. I'm writing this over the course of two to three years, and the only reason is because I need to give myself time away from my own mind. The more I write, the more I think and the more I judge myself. The way that I battle against this is to write what is on my mind, and the moment I lose a little courage, I take a break. This may sound lazy, but it is what keeps my passion strong and keeps me writing. That way, when I come back to the last instalment that I wrote, I forget what I have written and I can either wow myself or think it is awful and delete it.

Giving yourself room to take a break, and only allowing yourself to really succeed when you are truly you, is something that really helped me move on this year. I not only tried to stop caring about what others thought, but I stopped trying to always justify to myself that my actions were right. I encourage you to give it a try and let yourself be the authentic you.

Losing Someone You Love

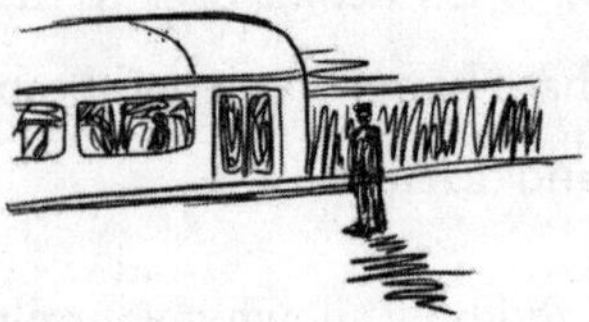

You seem to find every cloud on a sunny day

Hit every red traffic light on the road

And no mirror leaves you satisfied

Because losing someone isn't about death

It is about living in a world that moves on without them

The World Is Against Me Today

I woke up today and felt like nothing was going right, and I went through my entire day feeling angsty and mad at the world and whatever it was throwing at me. And I could sit here and explain to you how it was not my fault and the world has it out for me, but that is false.

Yes, sometimes we all have an off day. Things just don't go right, things break, things don't fit, and you just get fed up. But the tough realization is that I actually knew I was going to have a bad day. I remember my mom telling me that if you think negatively, your life will be negative. And then I hear that from every motivational speaker and I roll my eyes. You see, I am the type of person that has to fuck up to learn. I know it is not the best way to learn, but it has worked for me since day one. I broke a few bones, but hey, I learned.

I knew that I was going to have a bad day today because last night I went to bed thinking I was going to have a bad day. I ended my night yesterday on a little bit of an off note, and I carried that with me till my head hit the pillow. And I stayed up for hours upon hours, thinking that if I just kept scrolling on my phone, I could get rid of the thought.

The thought never went away.

I woke up the next day and had a fucking shit day. If you think there is math in life, that there's a perfect formula, then let me explain this differently.

Do negative + Think negative = Live negative.

I am not here to tell you that I know how life works, because I clearly don't. But life tends to surprise me and be easier and easier than I always thought it was; we just make it hard for ourselves. I am not talking about the specific life you live, or the place you reside, or your job. I cannot control that. I am talking about what is in your head and what you decide to tell yourself is true. You have the power to control how bright of a day you have, even if your surroundings are dark.

Long story short, the world isn't against you. You are. So shut up, and have a good fucking day.

Don't Be That Person & Give Up

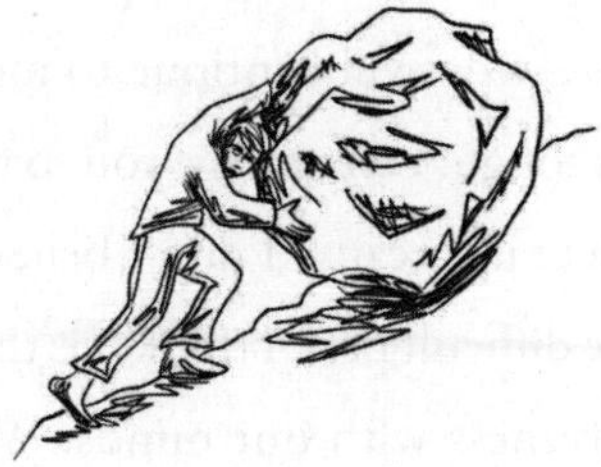

We all know the type of person I am talking about—the one that says they will do something and gives up the next day.

I didn't mean to call you out like that...

I have been very into working out lately and trying new challenges, and at first, I would try until it got hard and then just give up. I would go until the point where I had to push, where the task became a challenge. I worked out twice a day, every single day, for seventy-five days straight, and the hardest moments were at three weeks in and at the last week of the challenge. I am not saying all this to brag about how much better I am than the average person;

don't worry, there is a point to this. I think the reason I almost gave up in those two moments is because it was easier to let it go than it was to continue. The door was right there when the challenge just became a little inconvenient, and it was easier to give up than it was to go out of my way and work harder.

However, I stuck with it and I kept going and I am so fucking thankful that I did. We tend to surround ourselves with good people, but I think we need to go a step further and surround ourselves with people who will continue to move forward in life even if the path gets tough. I encourage you to find a challenge for yourself and complete it, because I don't believe that the specific challenge itself is the difficult part; I think it is the success or failure aspect that tends to mess with our minds. When we challenge ourselves to something, we don't necessarily have a consequence if we don't complete it, and that is why we tend to give up. Because . . . why not?

Stop thinking of your life as something you need to win, or that you could be spending your time on something better. Sit down, take out a pen, and write down who you are and what you want to accomplish. I am not asking you to write your life story or who you want to be in seventy years; just write something down and value yourself. Show your damn worth because I am tired of us being known for not being good enough. You are good enough, you are strong enough, and you can beat anything you put your mind to.

The most powerful person isn't the one with the CEO in front of their name or the one with the most money in their bank account. The most powerful person is one that keeps going no matter the obstacle in their path. The one that is their own biggest fan. The one that hustles on the days when no one else wants to push. The one that actually fucking cares. And it sounds like a pain in the ass, but guess what?

If it was easy, everyone would already be doing it.

So today is the day to stop being known for attempting a million different things and be the person that gets it done.

I Stopped Looking In Mirrors

There are not many things that I can say to make you feel okay, because I am similar to a mirror. I cannot reflect how you feel because I am not you. Growing up, I would avoid every single mirror I saw because I realized that I never looked the way I felt.

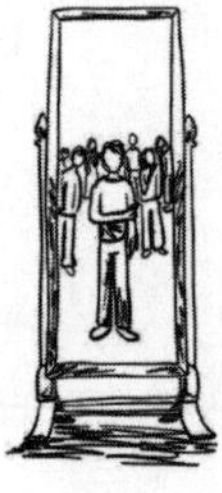

I felt unhealthy, lazy, tired, and depressed, but when I looked in the mirror, I would see someone skinny. The "goal" of society. But I never felt fulfilled, because alongside that "goal", I was called anorexic, and I was told that I needed to eat more. It made me hate the person that I saw every time I looked into a mirror.

So next time you look in a mirror, don't.

Not because you don't deserve to see how you look.

Not because it is going to lie to you.

Not because you should be running away from an issue.

But because I believe we should base our appearance off the way we feel.

When we look in a mirror, we see a reflection. A view of how others see us.

And if I'm being honest, you have done enough for everyone else. It's time you do something for you.

You Are Not Lost

Every so often, I have these moments where I want to go off and just be alone. And at first, I thought it was because people didn't want me around, or that I was lost or that I didn't fit it or that I just wasn't good enough.

But I realized that this was me needing a recharge.

I would go to a party and only be there for an hour and randomly leave without saying bye because it got too much. And I always thought it was bad, but I'm here to remind you that there's no rulebook to how you live your life. Yes, you have a path, even if it doesn't feel like it, and you're doing fine, but you're also allowed to take a break and stop and look around every once in a while.

So all in all, you're not lost. Your body is just reminding you that you need some time to better yourself instead of always putting others first.

Nice Guys Don't Finish Last

It has gotten to the point where the world is filled with the "nice guys" that complain about not being chosen. The common thought is that girls seem to want and choose the "bad boy." This has been grinding my gears lately because I once told myself I was one of the guys that never got chosen because I was too nice.

As I sat in my room depressed, watching romantic comedies and dreaming of finding someone who I could pass that love onto, I would think about how I was too nice and how no one would choose me. But as I have aged, dated, loved, and gotten my heart broken, I have realized that pity isn't good enough to fall in love. That may sound quite tough on myself, but it is the sad truth. This trend of feeling bad for yourself so that others will want to fall in love with you just starts to be sickening. It is time we stop this cookie-cutter shit and just be honest, because we don't have a lot of life to live.

Nice guys don't finish last. Having so much love to give, wanting to shower someone with affection, constantly wanting a conversation, and searching for someone to fill the void that is in your life is not the reason you can't find love.

If the reason you are dating is to find someone to display all your "nice guy" attributes onto, then you are dating for the wrong reasons.

Love Is a Scary Thing

Love is kind

Love is bare

But love with caution

Because it can leave a mark

That tends to scare.

The Off Day

A day off? Never heard of it. However, an off day seems to be my best friend lately. What's the difference? Well, a day off is a full break from work, or whatever consumes most of your time. An off day is when you wake up and just cannot figure out why you feel so shitty. And when you have an off day on a day off . . . well, then it just gets really unlucky.

I am twenty-five years old as I am writing this, and I believe that this is the most common age where people usually have the majority of their life together; whether it is having their career path planned out, having a house, getting their investments right, or even just knowing their daily routine. I am this age, and I do not have any of this. So the ultimate question is am I happy? Because I think that the reason we strive to have all this completed by that age is so that we can live a happy life with no worries.

Well, I am happy—that is, if I am not having an off day. I love having a good day of work where everything fits into the schedule just right and I eat good meals, exercise well, and consume lots of water. But when I wake up and have an off day, then the rest of my day kind of goes down the toilet. When this happens, the main thing that my manager and those around me recommend is to take a day off. But when I take a day off, I feel off because I don't feel the purpose of anything, but in reality it is what I need. But sitting on the couch, I ask myself, "Why? Will this benefit me today? My body is sore from sitting here, I would rather it be sore from running." I constantly find myself in my head on these days, and if I am not there, then I am on my phone.

We find ourselves in this weird routine of trying to find a routine, feeling like if we don't have one then we can't go on about our day. This leaves us on our phones, scrolling and trying to see what other people are doing, which ultimately leaves us in our heads for the remainder of the day.

It really isn't that hard to understand why we aren't motivated. We get more caught up in the idea of living a good life than actually living it. So how the hell do we find the balance?

I'll tell you this—it is not some magical routine you'll find online. It is understanding what you value in your life. No morning coffee, journaling session, or 5 a.m. wake-up is going to find that for you. Now, with that being said, it is important to try things, so I recommend expanding your palate when it comes to routines, but the way people create these is by doing things they love.

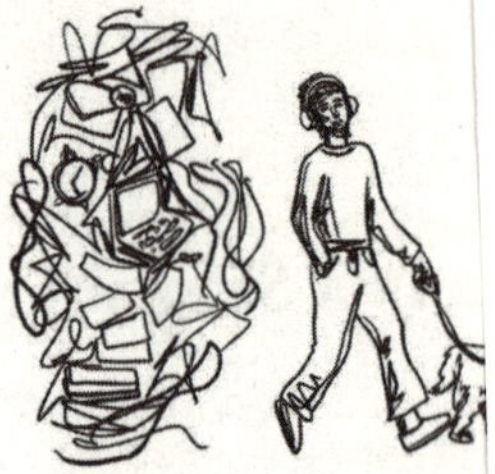

So if you like picking up a morning coffee, but it makes you late on your way to work, buy an espresso machine and make it at home. Who knows, you may love the process. If you want to run every morning, but the weather is too unpredictable, get a treadmill. If you want to journal every day, but you don't know what to write, then just m to-do list. There will always be ways around something an not saying that is a short cut, but you need to understand that single person's life is different than the next, even if you wo same job. We are all different people that enjoy different thin stop waking up at 5 a.m. if you don't like it and replace it shit you actually like. Then maybe, just maybe, you might act enjoy waking up the next day to go to work.

Personally, I hate days off, so I am not going to take them I am going to lighten my load each day. This way I am ab give myself some wiggle room to do the exercise that I want go out for lunch or on walks with my dog. But for fuck's sa am not living my life wrong just because it doesn't look good YouTube video. Live your life for *you,* and make it so that a day is something manageable rather than damageable.

Learning to Shut Up

I first started social media when I was sixteen years old on an app called "GifBoom." It was basically Instagram but instead of photos, you could only post gifs. It sounds very silly, but it is where it all started. It then gravitated towards Instagram and YouTube and, well, here we are. For context, I am now twenty-five years old and I have 458k followers on Instagram and 2.7 million on TikTok. I don't mean to be that guy that always brings up numbers and wants to talk about stats. I also do not want to bring numbers into a book that is permanent when there is inevitable change. But I believe numbers are destroying our lives and we need to talk about it.

Three years ago, I was in a very dark place. I was only posting content on YouTube, really depending on every single video to blow up in order to be paid in AdSense to then pay rent. The number beside my name was quite large, but that didn't translate on my bank statement as well as people might think. Now, it is not all about money, but when it comes to your full-time job and paying rent, money seems to matter. Alongside this, I was depressed, more anxious than ever, and the suicidal thoughts were rushing through my mind. I posted a video called "I filmed my anxiety attacks for a week" and it got millions and millions of views. It truly saved my channel . . . at the time. People were constantly asking me for advice on anxiety as if I was a therapist, but in reality I was just a kid facing it myself.

Long story short—because I hate talking about myself as if it is bragging—I've been really depressed for the past three years. I found myself in this bubble that I could not pop, and I felt that if I gave up my social media job, then I was a failure and everyone could see that. Not just my mom, or my girlfriend, but the entire world. I started to share my thoughts and feelings and posting videos, tweets, and stories every single time I had a new one pop into my head. I stopped living and I started sharing . . . everything. I became open to talking about the most personal topics and sharing them with the world in order to get people to keep listening to me. And when not enough people were listening, I would feel the need to come up with a better story, or a harder heartbreak. I began to be the most toxic thing in my life.

Then I shut up.

It doesn't get more simple than that. I found myself always wanting to share, share, share, and I got to the point where I had nothing more to give the world; I ran myself dry. So, I stopped talking. I started listening to myself rather than the comments on my computer screen. I still shared my thoughts, but I collected them first rather than blurting them out as soon as they came to me. I wrote them down, I sat with them, and even if they were great thoughts, I kept a lot of them to myself. Not everything is meant to be shared, whether it is with a loved one or the world. Some things are meant for yourself and for you to feel and keep inside.

At that point in my career, I was ready to give up. I knew that this silence is what I needed for myself to keep going, to stay alive and to stay strong. And then I started sharing things that I have already written from my books, my notes, and my journals. I stopped trying to constantly create content and I started to repurpose it. I fell into the groove that every thought and emotion I had was something that was meant to be shared and it became toxic to my life. And I know this may not be as relatable as the other instalments, but it is the one that has saved my life. I encourage you to learn to shut up and live for yourself rather than for the story. Whether it is Instagram, Twitter, YouTube, or even a post on Facebook, I promise you it can wait. Your life is a greater story than any given moment that you have experienced. You are still welcome to share those thoughts, feelings, and experiences, but please promise me that you will live it and process it on your own before you let others deem if it is good enough.

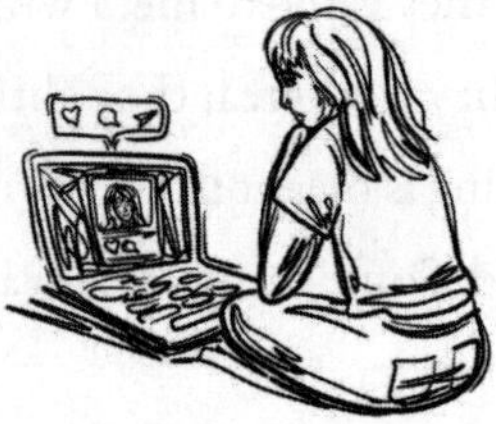

You are good enough, your voice is good enough, and your life is good enough. So please stop talking and start living, because you just might enjoy it a little more.

Since this moment of realization, I choose specific content that I share with the world, and other thoughts and feelings remain within. Not only has this changed my outlook on life, but it has changed my career, and I am happy to say this is the most successful and happy I have ever been. And hell, I am so proud.

Girls Are So Complicated . . . But So Are Guys

I have heard it many times, and it doesn't seem to be a phrase that is going to go away anytime soon. Whether it is my guy friends or my girl friends, they are always complaining how the person they want never seems to want them at the same time. One moment they are in love, and the next it seems to fade. One day they are texting non-stop, and the next they can't seem to even get a reply. So they stop texting and then lo and behold, the texts start coming in.

So what is it? What is the deal here?

Well, to be honest, I don't actually know because I am not that person, but I do have an idea or two. The first possibility is that they just don't like you, they dislike you, they utterly despise you. A little harsh? Yeah, I thought so too, but hey, it is a possibility and it is not to be ignored. Sometimes we are a little ignorant to the fact that there are people out there who may not like us, how we act, or even just something that we said.

Now, let us go to possibility number two. They like their alone time and you're too much. Harsh again? Yeah, this time I don't think so. Have you ever found yourself annoyed by your parents, and they leave you so frustrated? Or been spending too much time with a close friend and now certain quirks and traits they have just seem to piss you off? Don't worry, you are not an asshole. I am the same way, but I figured it out, at least for myself. We all need our alone time to think, rest, and most importantly, recharge our batteries. So when someone is constantly texting you, or you're in the beginning of a relationship and your partner is always touching you . . . well, that can be a little overwhelming.

When you give someone your all, when you give someone everything that you have, then the chase has come to an end and they stop running after you. And this is not a bad thing; it just means you have to find someone who is living life at the same pace as you.

And don't go crying, trust me. They are out there.

Two Year Anniversary

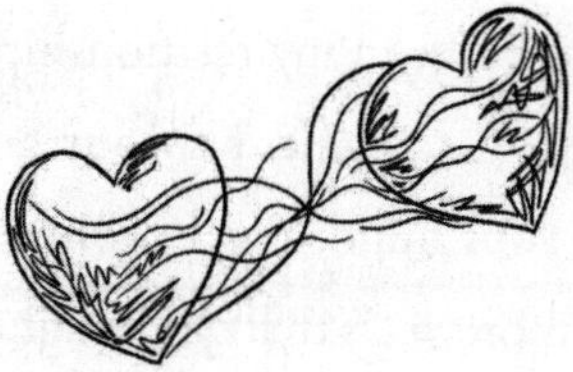

A place in my life that I can honestly say I never thought I would see at one point. My first love was followed shortly by my first heartbreak, and I was left feeling completely broken. But it goes much further than that; I felt useless, I felt like I didn't belong on this earth, coffee lost its taste, and my cologne started to become unscented. No matter how many times I tried to "get back out there," it was followed by the darkest thoughts that personally attacked my feelings. And I word it like that because I want you to know that every single heartbreak that someone goes through is different. No two heartbreaks are the same.

I finally reached my two-year anniversary with my girlfriend and I am grateful. It is something that is very difficult to describe because it took a lot of pain to get through, and it honestly feels like a relief at this point. A pat on the shoulder, if you will. This may not be the greatest thing for my girlfriend to read, but to those out there that are facing a heartbreak and thinking that love was only meant to enter their life once . . . well, I don't want to say that you are wrong, but I do encourage you to be more open-minded. People come into our lives for a reason, they leave for a reason, and they stay for a reason. And I know you are reading this thinking I am going to tell you the reason, but how could I possibly do that when each person is so vastly different?

I feel grateful, proud, happy, and strong to be in my relationship for two years, and I am sure there are more to come. I encourage you to love with your heart instead of your mind, and I promise you that love will be all around you in more ways than you might have imagined.

Everyone Has Something Bad to Say

This idea of a perfect person with a perfect past and a perfect future is a fictional character that we all seem to believe in. These past few years, we have seen a lot of "cancel culture."

Cancel culture is when people try to end someone's career because of something that they have done, said, or an action that happened in the present or past.

From tweets, to old Facebook posts, to things caught on video, we have immediately felt the need to try and end someone's career or life because of a mistake that they made instead of making it a teachable moment. Now, I want to preface this by saying that I couldn't possibly know which *cancel culture* situation has come to your mind while reading this. You may be thinking I am an asshole for trying to justify helping someone when they have done something poor in their past. I am speaking on this in more of a general way.

I think we need to be better people when it comes to accepting the fact that people fuck up. Granted, you do have your fair share of people that make mistakes and remain unapologetic about it and continue to make the same mistakes. They aren't searching for your forgiveness so it is time to move on from them. I have messed up many times in my life, I have grown up differently and acted differently than I do in my life now. You can read this as an excuse, but I believe that we have too much hate in our hearts.

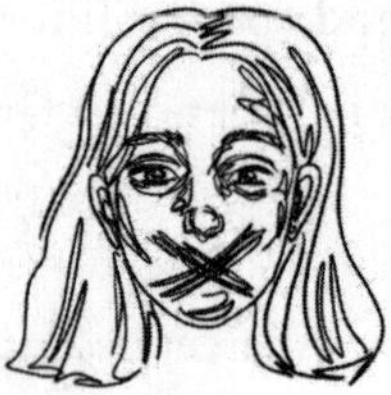

Have you ever hung out with a friend and they begin to gossip about another person in the friend group? Of course. We have all been there, and we have probably been the one who was gossiping as well. I am not here to burst your bubble of perfection, but have you ever thought that if your friend is gossiping about someone else, who's to say that they aren't doing the same about you?

I bring these topics up not to make you feel like shit but maybe to think/look at some situations in life a little differently. Before you cancel someone or gossip about them, just simply ask if you'd like that to be done to you. There is no way to be a perfect person, but seeing the other side is never a bad thing. I always thought that I was an awful person because if a crime was committed, I would want to know why instead of immediately hating on the person. Obviously what they did was wrong, but I can't live my life without knowing why. It not only interests me, but it helps me understand.

To Anyone Going Through a Breakup

Why is it that even if you are in a happy relationship, you can always feel the pain of a past breakup?

I like to think this is love's doing.

This is for anyone going through a breakup and needs to add up all the thoughts in their head so that they start to make sense again. When someone we truly love leaves our lives, it feels like they take our life with them.

Our favourite coffees lose flavour, the scenic walks we used to take make us feel lost, our bed feels cold, our food tastes bland, our clothes don't fit, and our heads feel disconnected from our bodies.

If I just described how you have been feeling, even if it was just one thing, then I think that proves you aren't alone in your situation.

But for some, that would upset you to know. You don't want someone to be like you because for once in your life, you are able to feel something. Even if it is painful. You are processing this breakup as the worst thing that has ever happened to you, but if you haven't been able to feel lately, then maybe this breakup was the best thing. Someone leaving your life always sucks in the moment, but down the line, it all starts to make sense. I am not here to tell you that time heals all wounds, because you already know this. I am here to tell you that you have the strength to endure that time alone and find yourself again.

So why does this hurt?

1. You lost someone you love.

2. You let go of someone you love.

3. You feel nothing.

Now the obvious patterns will happen.

1. You will feel it heavily.

2. You will be angry.

3. You will work on yourself a lot.

4. You will use your body.

5. You will miss them.

So if we know all this, and we know that breakups and their outcomes are so common, why does it still hurt so much? Every single person is different, and so is every relationship, so allow me to share my personal experience.

Breakups hurt so much because you once envisioned an entire life with someone to the point where you lost who you are without them. And that is usually why couples tend to distance themselves because one partner loses who they are and becomes dependent on the other. And once the weight becomes too heavy, someone has to break. So you might think that you hate that person for breaking your heart, but a lot of the time, it comes from the feeling of letting yourself down. We create this picture perfect relationship in our minds that we need to see unfold and when it doesn't, it breaks us. Even if it was never meant to work in the long run, it still hurts.

And now that I just tore your heart into shreds, allow me to try and fix it.

I only got one for you here:

1. Ya just keep swimming.

It's tough shit, kid. But it is not the end of the world. If you wanted some cookie-cutter advice, you would have gone to your mom. I think what helps is to know the painful fact that your ex is already doing the same. The relationship ended. It is over.

It is time to learn who you are again, and be okay with the fact they will be doing the same.

And I have to say, congratulations. Because you made it this far in this instalment speaking on a subject that you feel broken about. And for that, know that you are strong enough for anything.

I'll see ya when you go through your next breakup.

Don't Lose Yourself in Love

Why do we fall in love with someone? It's not their money, that wouldn't be right. It's not their looks, that would be lust. It is for who they are. Their passions, hopes, dreams, and everything about their being. That is the beauty of love; it requires no changes. But oftentimes in relationships, there comes a moment when things start to get a little rocky. This is usually after the honeymoon phase, and it comes out once things start to get serious. The arguments start to occur over the littlest of things, and anger frustrates both people because they don't know what they did wrong. This is something that I have been through in each of my relationships, and it honestly broke the first one apart.

When we fall in love with someone, we fall in love with who they are. When someone falls in love, they fall in love with who you are. As we spend time with our significant others, we can notice ourselves saying their catchphrases, or taking after their habits, and even copying their mannerisms. It is at this point where we have lost who we are and lost ourselves in this relationship that we used to call love. But now the love is fading, because the person that you fell in love with, or the person that fell in love with you, has now changed. Now, change in life is inevitable, and both partners will experience it and hopefully be there for one another. But this type of change revolves around one person, and it takes place because a partner morphs into their significant other. The mannerisms, the language, the routines all become meshed into one person, and you are no longer in love; you are just coexisting with one another.

And when this happens, it kind of sneaks up on us. We don't know it is something we are doing, but we can feel the vibe of the relationship shift, and we believe it is because we aren't doing enough or that we did something wrong. But in reality, it is because you or your partner stopped being them, being who they actually are, and it leaves you feeling lost and alone. It can turn into intimacy issues or feel like a lack of love, but it isn't because you don't love one another. It is simply because one person has lost who they are—their passions, their goals—and you both formed into one person.

So how do we fix this? I believe the answer is to become more independent. Which can be a huge struggle for a long-term couple who has done everything together for years, or a new couple that is still very much new to love but being with someone all the time has become a little more difficult than they thought.. I believe that spending time alone can increase your love for your significant other because you aren't being watched or drowning in empathy.

This is a tough conversation to have because when brought up, it can seem as if you don't want your partner around, when what you truly want is to be able to love them more. So when you bring up this topic, be prepared to have the conversation and be mindful of how you word it. I do not believe that love needs to be stagnant just because someone is scared to have a conversation with the other, and if you realize that's what you're doing, then maybe there's another issue there.

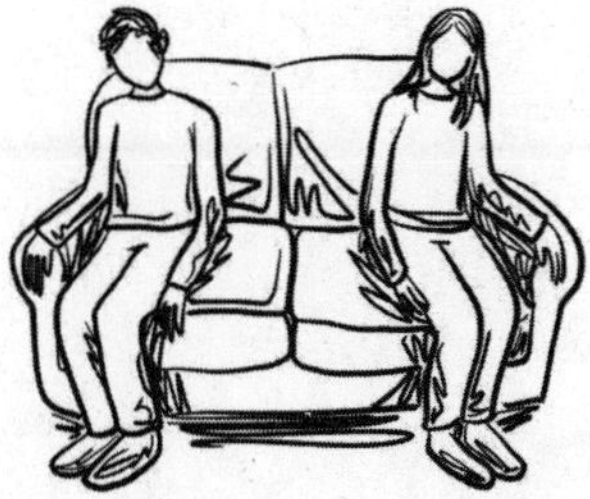

It is never wrong to want to love someone for who they are, but please do not get it mixed up with wanting to love someone for who they were. Because, like I acknowledged before, change is inevitable, but one of the reasons you fell in love with someone is their views on life and how they handle change and adapt to situations. In the grand scheme of things, if you truly love them and want to be with them, then the question of wanting your partner to be themself isn't that hard because ultimately you want them to be who they are for their own mental health. This will not only make the love stronger, but it will make each partner as independent as they should be. It means being okay alone, handling tough situations that they would've had to do before, and most importantly, being happy when no one is around. These aren't wrong things to want for someone. It will leave you feeling so much more appreciative of your partner because they are there to help when you need them, not just for convenience.

I Am Terrified of Success

It should all be getting better, right?

I should feel really happy?

I should be feeling fulfilled?

Well, I don't. And the only way that I can get my thoughts out is if I sit down and write them out and allow them to work their way out of my crowded head. A lot of this book is about sharing advice from what I have learned through emotions that I have felt during experiences that I have faced, except this one. For this instalment, I would love your input on this matter because it is something that I have been dealing with my whole life and maybe it is something that you can relate to as well. Maybe it is something that is confusing in your head, and you haven't found the right jumble of words to explain it.

Every single time I experience a glimpse of success or happiness in my life, I immediately think about how it can go wrong. Yes, this allows me to appreciate the moment that I am in—because once it is over, it is gone forever—but it really puts a downer on my mood. When I get a chance to replay this memory in my head, all I can think about is how it got messed up in the end. It is obviously something that I am working on, hence why I am writing about it. A huge issue I think people face is that when they are dealing with a problem, they don't even know where to start. I believe just thinking, assessing, and even writing down the situation can truly help lay it out so your brain can understand.

So, I think that I overcrowd my success with failure due to a sense of humility. I don't believe that it has everything to do with negativity even though it may sound depressive. Just because something is emotional does not make it sad. If anything, I think the ability to think about your thoughts, placing them in a separate category to emotions, is a true strength. It shows a sense of self-love, self-empathy, and that you genuinely want to handle the situation. Which is a tough spot to be in because a lot of us get addicted to the pain.

And if there is anything that I want you to take from this installment, it's that the way you think is never a thing to ignore. I know that the term "overthinking" has been drilled into our brains, but that is very different from processing the emotions that you are feeling. I hope you feel valued and validated by yourself before anyone else, even if you are a little frightened about seeing who you truly are.

Moving forward, I am going to allow myself to feel the benefits of success before I start planning how I am going to recover after failing. I am going to share it with my peers, family, and loved ones before I ruin every situation in my mind. I am going to allow myself to be me, feel free, and be fucking happy, even if it all comes crashing down in the end. At least when I replay the memory back in my head, I will be able to spark a smile.

Cry With Me

I want you to cry

Never alone

And always with me.

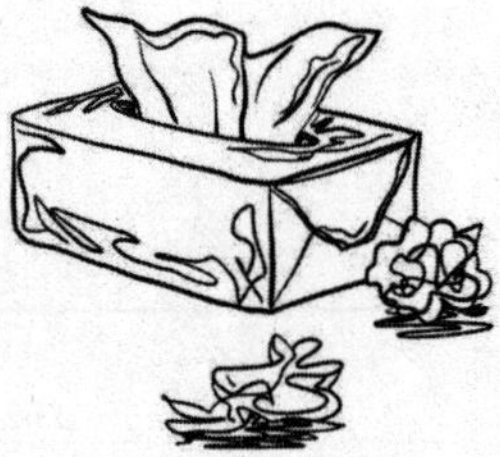

Dating Again Pt. 2

"Let's hope there won't be a dating again part two."

I really never thought that I would be here again, and it is not even that I am dating again, but it is the thought of having to date again that is crushing me.

January 24, 2022, was my loneliest day in years, and it was because I loved too hard. I envisioned the future too clearly, and I wasn't on the same page as the one I love.

The question that I ask myself is, "How do I know when to write?" and the answer has always been when I feel something and when I have no one to talk to. So I turn to my pens or my laptop, and I start rambling away until it all of a sudden starts to make sense. I began to find peace in these really dark moments where I thought I would be breaking down and crying. There is nothing wrong with crying, but it hurts in a very different way than what tears can portray.

The moment that I heard the words leave their mouth stating that they were feeling indifferent about the relationship, I didn't hesitate even for a second to comfort them. At the moment I did not feel hurt, I did not feel pain, sorrow, heartbreak, and I didn't even need to put it aside because it was nowhere in my mind. Those reading may think this is endearing, and at first I thought it too, but it is endearing for the one that is slightly breaking my heart. It took me years to realize that I am allowed to feel pain, and I am capable of it. And even though I've realized that, I have yet to put my feelings first or even remotely touch them when someone is in need.

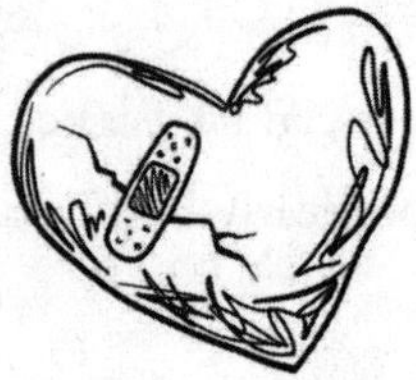

It is something that I am still . . . I was going to say "working on," but let's be honest, I am not working on it, because I haven't figured out how to do it without getting my heart broken and trying to find myself again. And I sure as hell don't want to have to go through another heartbreak or even a little sliver of heartbreak in order to try and work on it.

I'll update you more on how my heart feels once it is done repairing itself.

Heartbroken

Just because your heart is a little broken

Doesn't mean it stops beating when it

Comes to loving yourself.

Right Person, Wrong Time

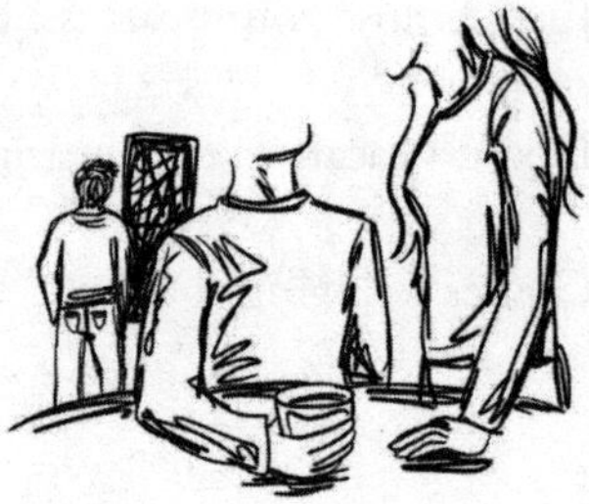

You can spend your entire life avoiding the question, but I encourage you to confront it—why aren't they here?

It's not because of timing. It doesn't mean that your love wasn't special, it doesn't mean you need to forget it and move on. And we can sit here and exaggerate this phrase, but I believe that people are in our lives for a reason. They are here for a reason, they leave for a reason, and we love them for a reason. And they break for a reason.

And whether we believe it or not, at that time we needed them.

And maybe now, we just need us. Or maybe there is no time.

If it's the right person, it just is. We don't have all our lives to waste on the negative *what if*. But we can turn it into a positive and think,

"What if it all works out when it is supposed to with who it is supposed to be?" The main thing you can do is prepare yourself.

Loved and Confused

In a previous instalment, I mentioned that my relationship went on a break. Can you guess how long that lasted?

About twelve hours.

But even though we are still together, can you guess how long the pain lasted?

It is still going.

Because I am human, and I feel things even though people think that I have all the right answers because I write things down in books. But that is how I find my answers—when I think my thoughts and take time to feel them. This is the exact reason I am still in pain because I never even got a chance to process that a break was needed, which means that I was part of the problem. It gets me thinking a lot about how, after a breakup, we still feel like someone owes us an answer—an answer that we may never get. Maybe it is closure that I am searching for, or maybe it is just that my heart broke a little and it is healing.

Confusing Love & Hate

Have you ever gone back to an ex or even thought of them in a blissful way, forgetting every reason why you two didn't work out? If you said no, then you either have never been in a relationship or you are simply a liar; heck, even I have! It's interesting how when we think about our own past, it can seem so negative, but when we think of a past lover, we think of all the connections we had with them. From emotional, physical, sexual and spiritual, these connections are what made us so in love with each other.

Now you are broken up and have moved on, but then a lonely night hits and you realize they are one text away. You are left contemplating if it is something you should or shouldn't do, and let's be honest, we all eventually send that text. Looking back on an ex is never a bad thing to do; it is just like everything else in how things are only good in moderation. We can get these flickers of love and hope in our minds where these moments together replay very vividly and we can easily get confused why we feel so much love for this person we thought we hated. But if nothing bad ever happened and you two just didn't work out, then how can you live your life hating someone you once loved?

You don't hate them; you are too good of a person for that. You hate that it didn't work out because you put effort into a relationship and it didn't give the return you were hoping for. Now, that can sound like a bank transaction when you read it, but it is a lot more than that. We go from living our lives for ourselves—going to college, studying, getting a job, having hobbies—to sharing an entire life with someone and doing everything together, always having them in your mind somewhere. In the next instalment, we are going to touch on closure, but I wanted to place this here so you understand that your feelings are valid. Moving on takes time, and it differs for each of us because no one person has had the same love in their lifetime, and that should not be overlooked. I hope you found peace in this, and when you are ready, the next page is ready for you.

Let's Talk Closure

Why is it that when the people we love leave, we still feel attached to them? For some reason, we just can't let go.

I think that is because you never got closure.

This is for anyone who is searching for an answer after going through a breakup, for those that need to add up the things in their head and take stock of what the breakup left them with in order to get closure. Oftentimes we are left thinking and feeling like we are the problem, or that we did something wrong, or that we weren't the person they needed us to be. And to be honest with you, those are all valid reasons, but if they don't sit right with you, then they're probably not your reason.

This person has left such a huge mark on your life to the point that you can't do anything without thinking of them—whether it is hatred for them, love for them, or just a wandering thought that doesn't really leave your mind.

When someone who we thought we would be spending the rest of our life with leaves, our entire world flips upside down. We are left with broken trust, canceled plans, and a person who has changed entirely from the person that we once fell in love with.

So why does not getting closure hurt so much?

1. You are left empty.

2. You think that you are the problem.

3. You can't stop thinking about them.

I know you are here for one question and one question only:

How do I get closure after a breakup?

I think sometimes the closure is the way they left. It told you everything so you don't need any specific words. Actions speak far louder than words in this situation. But if that is not you, then hopefully this helps:

1. Disinterest is your step to closure.

2. The lack of love is your step to closure.

3. The way they mistreated you is your step to closure.

I think oftentimes we search for closure and even if we stumble upon something that works, we are still left feeling empty because a part of us always wants to be searching for closure; it is the last piece of that person that we have.

Some days, when the thoughts replay in your mind, the way they pushed you seems playful, the way they argued with you seems like conversation, and the way they didn't love you seems like playing hard to get.

Because we don't want to let someone go. Why would we? We love them.

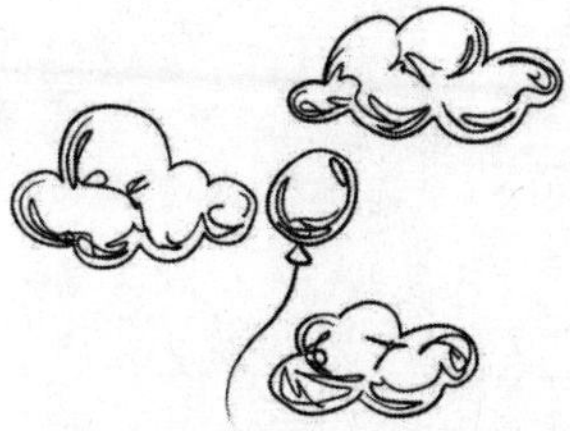

But they didn't love you. Otherwise they would be here. They would be holding your hand through any barrier you need to cross, whether it is being stressed at work, not being able to conceive, fighting with family, or battling a demon in your head. Them not being there, and shutting the door behind them when they left, is all the closure you need to understand that they aren't coming back. And you are going to be more than okay without them. You will learn to be strong on your own, to love new things, and to be a person that they never let you become. Don't let someone disappear and reappear in your life, because it will go by faster than you think, and you will be left searching for closure your entire life.

The more you search for this closure that is nowhere to be found, the more you are opening a door to fool you that they love you. When in reality, there is no closure. Because they left. And that has to be good enough to move on. Because you deserve it. And I am proud of you for making it this far into an instalment on a topic that breaks you. It means you are one step closer to moving on.

Life Upside Down

For the last three days, I have been running on empty. My life got turned upside down for the better, and I have felt like I have been awake for seventy-two hours. With that being said, it has already given me a life lesson that I believe can be applied to everyone. For a little more context, I got last-minute notice that the landlord of the home I am currently in is selling the house. Moving out was something that was always on my to-do list, but I had been planning for a time span of six months to a year, not two months. The thoughts that I had about moving out was to purchase a home so that I could get started on my future, but there were a lot of things that needed to be aligned before making such a big purchase. My relationship is still in the foundation-building stage, my job is still unstable, and being a first-time home buyer, there are a lot of questions that I do not know the answer to.

So what is the lesson I have been learning? There is no amount of sorry that someone can say to make you feel any better. While this situation isn't do or die, and it is not anywhere near a disaster, it is still a big challenge in my life. So I did something that I never do and I asked my friends for advice. Every single one of them apologized that I have to go through this situation and it got me thinking. It was very touching, and it did mean something to me, but what I noticed was that it did nothing. The challenge was still present, I still needed to move out, find a home, buy a home, figure out money, not to mention all of the questions I did not have answered. However, I learned that there is no one that is going to get things done other than myself. And I can apply this to anything in my life—doing my taxes, taking care of my dog, feeding myself, even taking care of myself every day. No matter how many times someone apologizes, shares their condolences, or tries to help, you will still need to be in control and handle your situation.

This doesn't mean that what your friends have said is invalid, or that it didn't mean anything to you. I honestly felt amazing after asking my friends for advice because I didn't feel alone, and it came across that they could feel my pain. They offered to help me move, a place to stay, and many alternatives that definitely meant a lot to me. But I am an adult now, and this is not something that they can teach you in school or a moment that your parents can prepare you for. I remember when my parents went through a struggle, I would just assume they would solve it, that it was an easy answer. No matter how many times they explained how complicated it was, I never understood. Now that I am in this situation where all the answers lie within, I am the only person that can take action. There is no one who is going to push me, do it for me, or yell at me when things need to get done. It's up to me, and as defeating as it may sound, for once in my life I feel powerful. I may be running on three hours of sleep, but I do not feel weak. I have control over my life, which is something that I never felt growing up, and even though it is terrifying, something about it is comforting.

There is obviously more to my circumstance than I care to share, but my life is facing a big change, and I am more than stressed and excited to make it. Please let this be your reminder that you are the only one who has control over your life.

Anymore

You don't love me like you used to anymore.

And I don't think I want you to pretend anymore.

Hate Me

You can hate my guts

If it helps you wake up.

So How Am I?

Over the past few years, I have done a lot of growing with very little pain felt. I have been in a relationship with a very beautiful girl and it has been the hardest thing I have ever had to go through. I know you immediately think that this sounds awful, but when they say that relationships take work, they mean it. Your entire future is a person that is in front of you, and every corner of your mind is yelling, "Don't fuck up!"

You feel a little under pressure.

The longest previous relationship that I had was a year and a half. I am now going into three years in my current relationship, so this is completely unknown territory to me. The house, baby, and future talk has begun, and I am absolutely terrified. I feel unprepared. I don't feel good enough. I feel like they might not be good enough. I feel wrong. I feel right. There are days where I feel confident and ready, and there are days where I feel like an escape plan is desperately needed.

Now, I know this sounds awful, but society has really put on rose-coloured glasses when it comes to relationships. We all know that it isn't picture perfect, but it is even worse than that. You are taking two human beings—people that have grown up differently, function differently, and think differently—and putting them in the same room twenty-four seven. If this is something you can't understand, imagine being in the same room with your parents for twenty-four hours.

Yup, exactly. Now you get it!

You still love them, you still care for them, but at the same time you want to just run away and escape. From all of the growth that I have done over the years, the one thing that I have learned is how important alone time is. We often devalue it and think we should spend more time with people because we feel guilty if we don't. And just because your partner doesn't understand their own self-love, does not mean it is your job to figure it out for them and sacrifice your own. They are just as much a human as you are, and they will figure it out alongside the love that you are able to give them. Your alone time can be anything from going for a run, sitting in a room with headphones, going to a coffee shop alone, or—my favourite—going grocery shopping alone. I don't know why, but the grocery store is my happiest place in the world because there are endless opportunities to bring happiness with all the food, new snacks and strangers. There is so much advice telling people to start saying no if you don't want to go out, but that same advice can be applied to your relationship. Your health matters just as much as theirs, and if they constantly make you feel guilty for taking care of yourself, then you need to ask them what their priorities are.

So how am I? I am good. I just have a lot more growth to do, and I need to figure out how to do that without damaging the person I love. I just hope they love me enough to stay while I do some self-construction.

Unloving You

Learning to unlove you took me years

Trying to forget your favourite coffee shop

The food you loved

The movies that made you cry

And the way you made me feel even if I only saw you across the room

It took me years

And it took you what seemed like seconds

Because you fell out of love with me while you were in love with me

The look you gave me slowly started to fade away

You didn't enjoy your favourite food

You didn't laugh or cry at movies

And your phone gave you more dopamine than my kiss ever could

Learning to unlove you took me years

It took you seconds because you were doing it all along and didn't have the decency to tell me

The Lonely Side to Love

The one thing that nobody ever seems to mention is about how lonely the act of falling in love can be. It either seems to be so happy or so heartbreaking, as if there are only two sides. But when we are falling in love with someone, there is no one there for us, not even ourselves. We are so out of our bodies falling for someone in this honeymoon phase of love that we lose sight of who we are and who we want to become. Even though your partner is there, even though they make your day and hold you when the days are tough, sometimes it is not enough.

Because there will be those days when you break down. The ones where no one else matters, when there is nothing that someone can say or do because it all just seems to pass right through. These are the days where we need ourselves, but it is hard to find out where you are when you have been hiding for so long. With all that being said, please know that these days are important. In fact, these are the days where I truly feel the most connected with myself.

When it comes to feeling connected with ourselves, it usually happens when the dark times come. We fall in love so blindly, and oftentimes it is not planned. We have no idea where it is headed, but we are enjoying the journey. We think that the problems get easier, the issues will work themselves out, that we will always love our partner and that they will always feel the same. But when it all comes crashing down, it is the moment when you realize that you have been alone this entire time. You were just possibly distracted by someone who convinced you that they loved you.

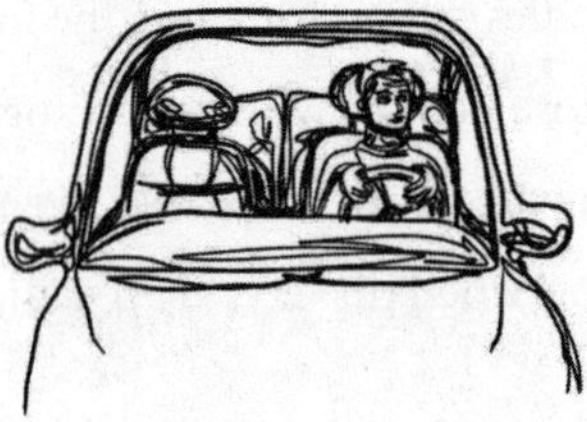

Now, you can take that to heart, and you can think that they did you wrong and hate their guts. Go for it! But I can't think like that, not yet. I think we did ourselves dirty by not checking in. I am not writing this because my relationship is ruined or a girl broke my heart. I am writing this because I feel alone in love, in my friendships, and in my life. This is me checking in with myself and reminding myself to not be scared just because I had a thought that hasn't been talked about. This idea that everything will always be okay, that if it is the person we love then it will all work out, is a little naive. Life takes a hell of a lot more work than that, and so do relationships.

Dear Reader Pt. 3

Just because you are thinking thoughts that aren't necessarily on the lighter side of things, or you are writing about the certain aspects of your relationship that you are not proud of, does not mean that is solely who you are. This idea of keeping everything bottled up and not letting anything out only leaves us feeling like we are full of lies. There are things in this book that I was absolutely terrified to write about because of how it may make someone feel, but I wouldn't be my true self if I didn't include it.

When you are in a situation where you have thoughts that are overflowing in your mind and have nowhere else to go, I encourage you to write them down. I know telling others can feel really good, but the reason why I don't is because I want these feelings out of me without having to replace them with someone else's thoughts and opinions. I think opening up to people is a very good skill and task to do, but please let yourself process your own thoughts before spilling them onto someone else. Writing allows you to strategically choose words to help explain what you are going through. I know your mind is tired, and you feel like you can't think these thoughts for one more second, but the moment you start writing about them is the moment you perceive them differently.

That time when someone broke your heart, maybe once you start writing about it, you will realize that you wanted them to break it so that you didn't have to break theirs. Maybe the time your partner forgot to make you a cup of coffee in the morning really made you feel that they didn't think of you, and that is okay. The way that we translate the thoughts from our mind to the words on paper can truly help explain situations to us. They could go from worse to better, and they very well could go from amazing to the worst thing in the world. That is a sacrifice that you are going to have to make, but I promise you will better understand yourself after doing so. You do not need to be an author to write a book, and you do not need to be a psychologist to know that replacing your worries with someone else's will only damage you in the long run.

So, to be clear, I am not telling you to bottle things up. I am not telling you not to speak to your friends about your problems. I am telling you to think, process, and feel the thoughts in your mind first before you put them onto anyone else.

You are capable.

Rebuilding Home

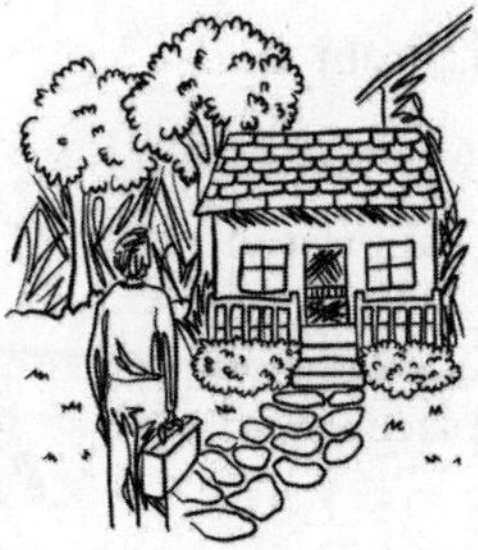

I look back on the past

In hopes to find any pieces I may have missed

To rebuild who I am supposed to be

And to remind myself why I exist.

FEELING LIKE YOU ARE NEVER GOOD ENOUGH

Imagine if every single thing you did, you second-guessed it. From sending a text, to becoming successful in your career path. The happiest moments are now a blur, and the exclamation point is replaced with a question mark.

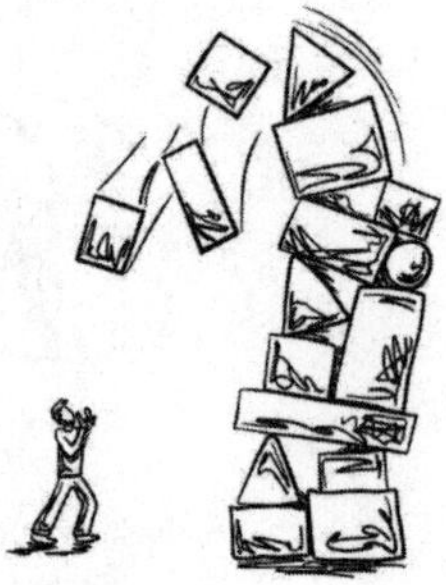

This is something that I have to live with.

The way that I like to live my life is not thinking that I need to change who I am, but needing to work with who I am in order to become stronger and to be able to see things with a more positive mindset. Two years ago, on a phone call with my therapist while I was pacing outside around my city, I was informed about my imposter syndrome.

So what is it?

Imposter syndrome is loosely defined as *doubting your abilities and feeling like a fraud.*

Every piece of success that I achieve, I feel like I did not deserve it.

Every love I feel makes it seem like they are better off with someone else.

And every breath I take makes me feel like my time could be spent doing something better.

So where does it come from?

Well, they say it usually stems from your childhood or parenting technique. So if you were really pressured to do well in school, criticized about every mistake, had controlling parents, or were constantly being compared to a sibling, then imposter syndrome might be something you face.

I also found out there are five types:

1. The Perfectionist – You focus primarily on how you do things, often to the point where you demand perfection of yourself in every aspect of life.

2. Natural Genius – If something *doesn't* come easily to you, or you fail to succeed on your first try, you might feel ashamed and embarrassed.

3. The Soloist – You believe you should be able to handle everything solo. If you can't achieve success independently, you consider yourself unworthy.

4. The Expert – Since you believe you should have all the answers, you might consider yourself a fraud or failure when you can't answer a question.

5. The Superhero – You believe that you should succeed at every role—friend, student, lover, parent, employee, etc. And when things don't come easy to you, your first thought is "this should be easier."

Do you resonate with any of these? Because even though these are labels, it doesn't mean that you need to put it beside your name or that it is assigned to you. Honestly, I must be a super imposter because I kind of experience all of the types.

But the moments that my imposter syndrome really affects me is when I am supposed to experience the happy emotion of success. For example, I have written two books and I have yet to celebrate any of them being published because I almost feel a pre-guilty effect.

I feel like I am not good enough because I didn't go to school to study how to write. Or I didn't grow up writing novels and reading until my eyes got tired. But I do love writing, and it is something

I have been doing forever, so I should be happy. But it isn't that I am not happy; that is what imposter syndrome hides. I *am* happy, but I feel guilty expressing that emotion.

Sometimes I get asked, "What is your biggest fear?" The first thought that comes to my mind is that I am terrified of becoming a successful failure.

I am so afraid to experience any form of success because I immediately think about how it could all go wrong. And then it loops back to how undeserving I am of this because if I was worthy of it, I wouldn't be thinking this way. But now that I have voiced how I feel and how it affects me, I know you might be a little anxious, especially if this resonates with you.

So here is how I live with it.

1. I acknowledge how I feel – I do this with my depression and anxiety, and it has helped a lot. Instead of stopping something, I try my best to understand why I feel that way and it helps validate myself.

2. Challenging my doubts – I like to think of this as mapping. If I find myself doubting success, I think of all the things that I have done in order to get there. I find writing an accomplishment list at the end of each year helps a lot.

3. Control comparison – We will never not compare our-

> selves to others. That is just not how we work, or how I work. So I think about their accomplishments of how they got to where they are. I accept their success, and by doing so, it disconnects them from me.

All in all, this is something that I still experience. I have imposter syndrome, and I can sit here every single day and think about it negatively, but I choose to look at it more as being humble. Which I know may not work for you, but it does for me. So to all my imposters out there, I encourage you to take a break every once and a while. Go do things that you loved doing as a kid, play a sport that requires your full brain capacity, and find your way of letting go. Because no matter how much you second guess, you should never question why you are here.

You deserve to be here, please remember that.

The Jealous Type

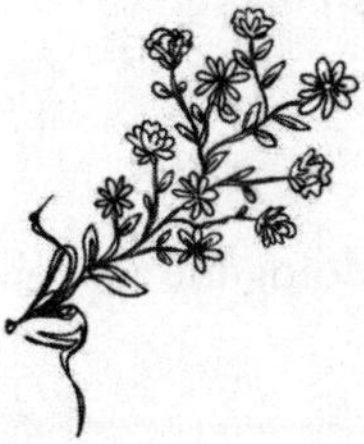

I am not the jealous type, but what I am jealous of is the truth when it's not spoken. This is usually hidden by lies because the other person thinks it is going to make you more comfortable to not know what is going on. They are wrong about this every single time.

The thing about the truth is even though it hurts, the act of someone opening up and being vulnerable makes up for the pain. The longer the truth is hidden from you, the more pain it can cause. Now, obviously there is no one reading this that is lying to their partner and is now going to confess their big secrets.

This is for those who have been lied to.

You are never wrong for telling someone how you feel, even if it is painful, and you are not worth any less just because someone doesn't have the emotional strength and the ability to put their ego aside to tell you the truth you deserve.

Falling Out Of love

If you're falling out of love with me

Just tell me

Instead of convincing yourself that you're doing me a favour.

I've Been Running Around All Day

I am sure this is a line that you have heard from either a friend or a partner, and it is usually said when someone feels stressed or that they can't do anymore. "I've been running around all day" is most likely a lie in reality but the truth in our minds. In reality, we have probably been scrolling on social media, skipping a routine to have a better start to our day, not eating or drinking right, and doing our normal activities. But they feel elevated because we are anxious, stressed, and we feel like we are out of control. And in our minds, we have been running around all day because we have been thinking about every single little outcome and possibility that something might have, whether it is a task we are doing or one that is in the future. It is one of those situations where we have quit before we have even started so that when it comes down to it, we have already thought about every single possible outcome of the situation.

If this is something that you find yourself saying, then I want to apologize for calling you out like that, but just know that you are not alone. This is something that everyone does, and it isn't until the aftermath that we realize we were stressed out to the max and did not help ourselves at all. So how do we realize it at the moment?

Slow down.

There is no chance of helping yourself if you are constantly in a rush because nothing will stick, and we are past the point of being naive enough to believe otherwise. If you are driving on a highway trying to look at the scenery, but you are going 120 kilometres per hour, there is no chance that you are giving yourself the opportunity to see everything. But at the same time, you cannot slow down because you need to do the speed limit and make it to your destination. However, it is the position that you put yourself in. If we are complaining about how we never have enough time, or we feel stressed and anxious and it is a repeating occurrence, then how do we expect it to randomly change one day? I will give you the answer right now: it will not. There will not be a circumstance where you condition yourself to handle the stress, because if it stresses you out each time, then it will stress you out everytime. The next drive that you go on, take the side roads and view the scenery. If we put ourselves in a stressful environment, we will be stressed out. And a nice little reminder: it is your life and you are in control.

The next time you say that you have been "running around all day," I want it to be literal.

A Moment

I could never sit here and lie to my-
self by saying you weren't the one

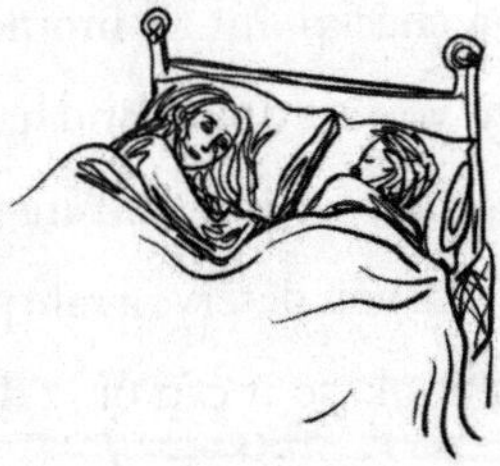

Or that you didn't make me feel
loved

Or that I wish I had someone else

Because there is a moment every sin-
gle day

When I look at you

And I can't help but feel grateful to have you by my side.

Checkpoint

We are nearing the end of the read, and I want you to allow this to be a checkpoint. A moment where you can breathe, ask yourself how you are doing, and have a moment of realization. I know there is something that you are thinking about at this very moment, and I think you deserve a safe place to let your mind wander. Now, this is a book, so it can only do so much, but how often are we really given a moment to think for ourselves? It always feels like we need to go out of our way to do it, and then when we finally do, we almost feel guilty because we have been running around (in our heads) all day.

This isn't a place for running, it is a place for you.

Lonely

You know when people say they want to be alone but not lonely?

I understand, but it doesn't make sense in my head

Because when I was sixteen

I didn't want to be alone

I wanted to be lonely

Because the thought of being alone and being lonely terrified me

And the thought of being surrounded by people and feeling lonely terrified me even more

You see, when I was sixteen, I wanted to be lonely

I always had trouble describing how I felt

Because I didn't feel anything at all

But if I was lonely

Then I would at least feel something

But if I was lonely

I wouldn't want to talk to anyone

But if I was lonely

I would know I feel something like someone else in this world

Because if I was lonely

For the first time in my life

I would be able to feel that I am here

Because no matter the space

No matter the people

No matter the friends or feeling equal

If I was lonely

I would at least know that I wasn't alone.

Why Do I Feel So Alone?

I haven't felt alone in a very long time, and I never realized how vicious of a cycle it could be. Looking at yourself and knowing that you'd rather be alone in this world and remain quiet is a hard concept to grasp. I am someone who finds a lot of peace in the quiet days, the ones where you can go an entire twenty-four hours without saying a word to anyone. I am not a person who really understands all the energy mumbo jumbo, but I definitely believe in it. I find I can sense the energy in the room no matter if it is sad, happy, neutral, anxious, or overwhelming. So to go an entire day without having to exchange or manage someone else's energy just starts to seem like a dream come true.

These quiet moments are not to be mistaken for rudeness or hatred towards anyone, because I know it can definitely come off that way. I don't blame someone if they think like that as well, because I basically become mute for a brief moment. Usually when it comes to this, it is because my energy levels are off the charts and I need to decompress. This is also very well known as burnout, but this is specifically the mental kind of burnout. It's where your mind and your brain become out of sync because you are trying to do things for others when you need to replenish yourself to get back to where you need to be.

When we are stressed, we don't function right.

When we are anxious, we don't function right.

When we are lonely, we don't function right.

And when all of these things are combined and we are living for someone else, we officially burn out the light in our hearts. And oh, my friends, I have not yet figured out how to start the fire again without absolutely shutting off, but I don't think it is a bad thing. There is definitely a way to do it without turning off the world around us, but the silence in our minds is key. Finding a place where we can be alone is so important—even if it is a crowded café, or getting our heart rate up while exercising so that we can feel the beat in our chest. The moment after you explode and start doing things for yourself again is the moment that you will find peace with where you are and be able to find your voice again.

Nothing Left to Give

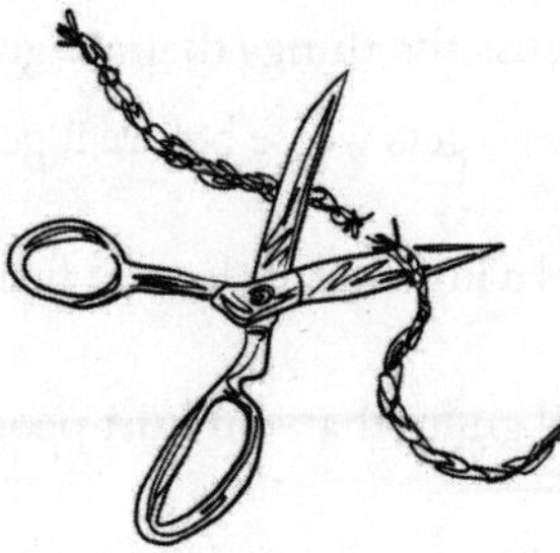

The title of this instalment already sounds too depressing, so I want to give a heads-up that it is more aggressive than depressive.

I have been there. Wherever you think you are, however alone you feel, I want you to know that I have been exactly where you are. Heck, if it is anything related to the title, then I am currently there right now. Your tank is empty, you feel tired all day long, and you feel unfulfilled.

Let's start this off with things that you need to understand when you feel like you have nothing left to give:

1. It is okay to say no.
2. Take time for yourself.
3. Stop making excuses.
4. It is okay to lose friends that don't want to be around.

And now that those all hit a little too close to home, let us go a little deeper and discuss the things that are going to suck. Yep, it gets uglier, but it always gets worse before it gets better:

1. You may feel a little more alone at first.
2. You may feel guilty that you hurt people by saying no.
3. You may feel even more lost because you made the decision to change.

But now it is time for it to get better for you, because it does! Like I said, this is not a depressive instalment, this is an aggressive one because of the lists, and it feels like I am yelling at you through my words. Here is the good list, the list of the things that I believe you need to do to get a little pep in your step:

1. Work out. Stop complaining about stress and doing nothing about it. Do something physical to take your mind off it, even if it is just going out for a walk.

2. Understand that you are here for a reason. The feelings you are feeling are there for a reason, and you feel like you have nothing left to give because it is time to move on.

3. Drink more water. I promise to drink more water. It will help.

4. Understand that it is important to express yourself.

Even though this part of the read has had a lot of points, it has also been very general; I did that for a reason. I want this to apply to anyone with any situation, because no matter how similar we all are, there will never be a situation that we experience exactly the same way; we are all different people with our own hopes, emotions, and experiences. So I hope this gave you the realization that you needed and hit home in the spot that you felt alone in, but I do have one more thing to say:

You are worth it. You are worth every thought, whether positive or negative, and you are worth every second of the day, every breath, and every sunrise. And I think it is time you find someone who lets you be that person, even if that someone is you.

Worst Pain

The worst pain is knowing they were

going to hurt you all along

And still giving them a

chance to.

It Never Ends How You Imagine

Much like books, the situations in our lives never end how we think they will, or they end exactly how we planned, but we always thought maybe it would change. This is the part about life that seems most interesting to me, because no matter how much we try, no matter how much we force something to happen, it always has its own way of working itself out. If you had told me this at the age of sixteen, I would have just shrugged you off and told you that the world was determined to make my life a living hell, but now I sit here as a twenty-six-year-old writing this book, and I am much more confident with this statement. I think it is partly because I am a little more positive and optimistic about life, but the other part is I don't have the strength to care. Because as we grow older, we care about different things, we worry about different things, we love different things. We also choose to spend our time on different things, and frankly, caring about how life turns out isn't one of them. With the amount of bills needing to be paid, people to take care of, possibly children to watch, there is just not enough time or emotional energy to change the world around us, and the greatest thing you can do is accept that it is okay.

It is not up to us how the world plays out our lives, but how we choose to live them.

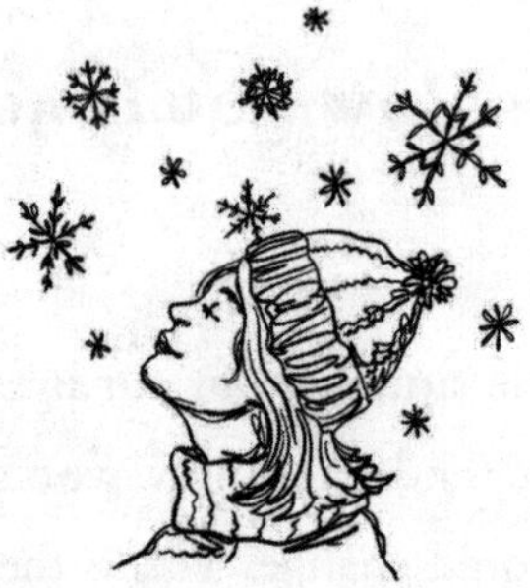

I Still Hate Them (Birthdays)

I turned twenty-six this year and I started writing this book when I was twenty-three years old. I love writing these books over a period of time because it allows me to notice the growth that I have made over the years, even if I haven't physically changed that much. What that gives me when I look back on my words is an exact emotion of how I felt. There is no acting like I can in a video, there is no fake smile I can make like in a photo; there are only the words that are in my mind at that moment in time.

Now, you know very well that I am not a fan of birthdays, and even as I have matured . . . well, I'm still not a fan. It is not that I don't enjoy being on this earth; it is that I don't believe I need one specific day every year to celebrate my life or to make others feel like they need to celebrate for me. I happen to live every single day like it is my birthday because I am grateful to be here, and as corny as it sounds, it allows me to actually be me. My mom always gets upset with me because she says, "I am the one who brought you into this world, and I deserve to celebrate your birthday," and I reply with,

"Mom, I celebrate the life you gave me every single day. Isn't that better than celebrating one day a year?"

I am not trying to downplay my own mother here, but I will never be the person who looks forward to the one day every year. I will never be the person who wants to feel guilty for others celebrating my life, and frankly, if they only feel like they want to acknowledge my existence on that one day, then maybe they aren't my friends. Now, that sounded a little harsh, but I do have a takeaway for you from this instalment.

Appreciate the life you have every single day, and please do not wait for a specific moment of the year to start or your life to change just because the number of your age does. Forget the year you were born, forget how you are supposed to act for your age, and forget about a one-day celebration. Live your life for how you want it to be, not how it should be, because one day you are going to turn an age that you won't like and all you will have to look back on is the question, "Why didn't I live in the moment?"

Dear Reader Pt. 4

Welcome to the near-end of the book! I hope you found peace and comfort during this read, and that it made you feel like you were able to connect the missing pieces in your head. You now know about my pain, happiness, struggles, hard times, happy times, and things that I have learned about life and myself over the past three years. You may think you now fully know me, but as I have mentioned before, you can never fully know someone because what lives in their head and what they put out into reality will never be a true reflection of who they are. My story continues, my life continues, and so does yours. I hope we are both able to grow in ways that are greater than our thoughts could ever imagine.

Every struggle, every mishap, every breakup, every date, every loss, every heartbreak—after it all, I am still here today, and I will still be here tomorrow, feeling thankful for how strong I have become. The thing that I want you to take away from all of this is how capable you are. It will get easier as it gets harder, and you will be more than okay.

Do Not Rush

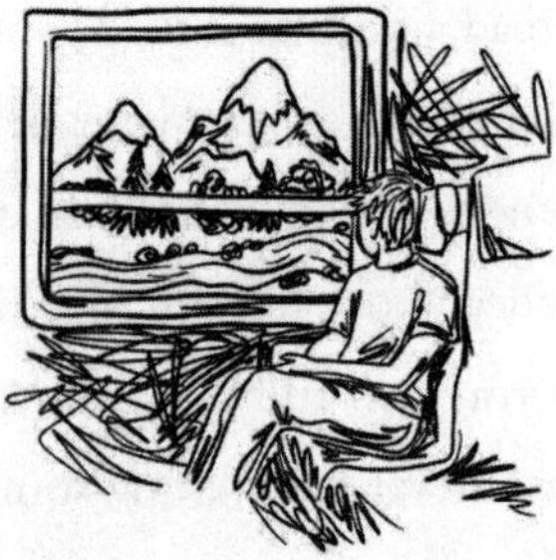

Please do not rush through this life.

You are exactly where you need to be.

And you are going at the perfect pace

To see everything in life that you are supposed to see.

How To Love Your Life

You are going to hate me when I say that it is all quite simple: stop doing the things you hate. Now, granted, I know there are a lot of things in our lives that we hate doing but are mandatory, like taxes or how we might get food on the table, and I know some are limited due to certain financial reasons. But there is no possible way that I can make this point and appeal to every single person, so I hope you apply this with how it fits your life right now.

In the last three years, I have noticed my happiness and my energy levels decrease immensely, especially when I was around people. I eventually figured out that I was giving all of my energy away to people who didn't make me feel fulfilled. I was doing things that weren't mandatory that made me feel useless, and I was wasting my time because I just didn't enjoy doing them. This could be as simple as waking up and eating breakfast right away because that is what I have learned. Or feeling rushed when I get ready for the day, and even if I have all the time in the world, I neglect that and start my day off feeling anxious. And the biggest one of them all is food. Instead of saying no or preparing ahead of time, I found myself eating out, ordering in, or consuming the foods that I know don't sit well with me and do not make me feel energized.

The change that you are waiting to hear does not lie within these words because they are different for all of us, and I know damn well that you have already thought about the change you want to make in your life. I am just wondering how long you need to think about this change before you actually do something about it. If you don't like the way coffee makes you feel on an empty stomach, stop drinking it on an empty stomach. If you don't like how much your neck hurts after a night watching TV stop sitting in the position and watch less TV. If you have the opportunity to change your job and you hate working there, quit.

Every single thing mentioned is easier said than done, but name one thing that isn't. Here's your reminder that this is your life and you should be living it to enjoy it. This is not one of those motivational alpha seminars telling you to hustle; this is just me telling you that you deserve better. Just remember that it is the simple things that make up our entire life, and if we change those to enjoy them, then we have a wonderful life ahead of us.

Take Your Time & Hurry Up

Why do we always feel so rushed? Even over the little things like getting ready for the day, making a coffee, being on time for a meeting, or going to bed. We constantly feel like we need to optimize our time while optimizing our productivity, leaving our issues, struggles, and our own well-being at harm. We are stuck thinking that we need to be waking up at the crack of dawn in order to be successful in our lives, only consuming coffee as we go about our days of feeling no emotion. Because if we felt anything, then it would stand in our way of this optimal achievement that we have created in our minds.

That is bullshit.

Life is not a morning routine that you see in a video online, it is not a specific order at your favourite coffee shop. Success is not determined by the hour in which you wake, and it is not the productivity that slowly deteriorates you. It is the fact that you are able to feel while you live. And when we fill our lives with the constant need to feel rushed, we will miss out on every emotion that we are meant to feel. The conversation about mental health has been more active than ever, but some of it comes alongside this fabricated version of self-love where you need to be a powerhouse of a human in order to succeed. And, granted, to be a successful person, you need to work hard, but you need to be mentally and emotionally capable to handle that stress before you venture off on the journey that will slowly kill you if you're not prepared for it. We all get to that point in our lives on a different timeline than others, and that is the perfect example as to why you should not be concerned about being on time to rush a life that is ending no matter what we do.

Now, that may be morbid for some to read, but it has helped me realize what is small in this lifetime and what I should not be wasting my life away on. This societal norm of self-love and the powerhouse of success is equivalent to someone saying *take your time and hurry up.* You are in no rush to get anywhere in life that you are not ready to be, because you are exactly where you need to be right now. This is not to say that you can't work towards something that you have always dreamt of, but it is okay to relax where you are. It's okay to have the dark days, the sad ones, and everything in between, because in order to get where you want to go, you need to be in one piece when you get there. If you are constantly rushing through life, you are going to forget to pick up your pieces along the way, because as we go through life, we will get damaged—through heartbreaks, death, loss, and emotional breakdowns—but it is nothing that we can't handle if we take our time to heal.

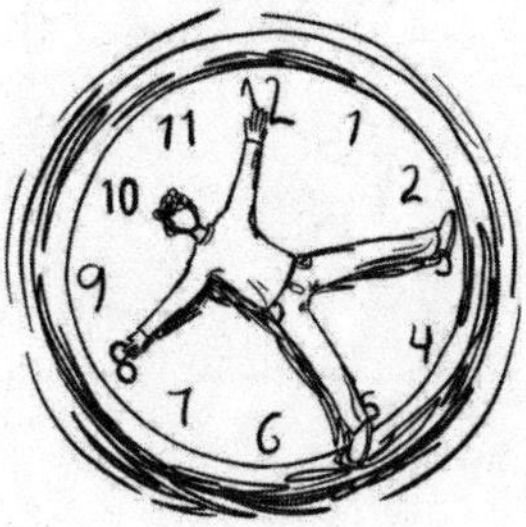

You will not be late, you will not miss out on a moment, and you will not need to catch up later. As we take the time for ourselves to heal, we are slowly becoming stronger in order to overcome this same issue in the future, because now we are more than capable of beating it. There is no battle in life that we magically beat the first time and are not shocked by; this is because our past barriers have all been hurdled by the act of recurrence. Whether it was an issue in our past that we faced, or it was something we emphatically felt from someone close to us, it gives us a little preview of what is to come, and we know that we are strong enough to face it.

You are exactly where you need to be, and you do not need to hurry up one bit.

You are capable.

You are strong.

You are the most perfect you.

And the only way you have achieved these traits is by living every moment of your life for who you are exactly meant to be, and that is you.

To Be Continued . . .

A Final Message To You

This book is dedicated to all of those with floating thoughts, broken hearts, lost souls, and who just want to feel heard. I know oftentimes we want to feel alone with our thoughts so that at least we are feeling something, but I am here to tell you that, though this book can be your own, I promise you are not going to be alone throughout it. I hope this allows you to find peace in your mind and connect the floating thoughts with words for them to make sense again. You have a purpose in this world, and that is to always remain who you are in every single thing that you do, so please do not forget to stay you. This book is written for you, by me.

Scan QR code to access the
Penguin Random House India website